MACROECONOMICS:

A PROGRAMMED BOOK FOR CANADIAN STUDENTS

MACROECONOMICS:

A PROGRAMMED BOOK FOR CANADIAN STUDENTS

D.A.L. AULD and E. KENNETH GRANT

Department of Economics

University of Guelph

PRENTICE-HALL OF CANADA, LTD.

Scarborough, Ontario

PRENTICE-HALL, INC., ENGLEWOOD CLIFFS, NEW JERSEY
PRENTICE-HALL INTERNATIONAL, INC., LONDON
PRENTICE-HALL OF AUSTRALIA, PTY., LTD., SYDNEY
PRENTICE-HALL OF INDIA, PVT., LTD., NEW DELHI
PRENTICE-HALL OF JAPAN, INC., TOKYO

Library of Congress Catalog Card No. 72-2477

0-13-542621-9

2 3 4 5 76 75 74

PRINTED IN CANADA

To Our Former Students

Baiba and Margaret

PREFACE

Economics is not an easy subject. But the comprehension of economics is of considerable value in understanding relevant issues in Canadian society such as unemployment, inflation, and balance of payments crises. The difficult aspect of economics lies in the unavoidably technical nature of the subject. Without this technical knowledge it is not possible to analyze properly the intricate interrelationships among the sectors of a relatively free enterprise economy like Canada's. The interplay of the household sector (which provides labour, consumes, and saves), the business community (which saves and invests), the government sector (which taxes and spends), and the foreign trade sector is complex; and any adequate understanding of the economy requires a basic analytical framework.

This book has been written to assist the beginning economics student in understanding some of the basic concepts and in manipulating the various techniques and tools that economists use to answer questions. It is only with an understanding of the technical nature of the economy that a citizen can critically evaluate economic policies and intelligently discuss present and future economic events in Canada.

The programmed learning approach is basically self-learning. It introduces the student to new concepts, and its structure is designed to allow the student to proceed at his own pace. Since the student is required to complete portions of the analysis along the way with the answers supplied at the bottom of the page, the problem aspect of programmed learning is self-correcting.

Combined with a standard introductory macroeconomics textbook, this programmed learning book may enable the student to assess his understanding of the material as it is presented in class. We would stress that a programmed book of this sort is not a substitute for a textbook; it should be used in conjunction with a good textbook. Hence, we have attempted to present a list of standard topics found in most texts.

In the United States, it was found after careful experimentation that the programmed learning approach was more successful than traditional lecturing approaches in teaching students the technical aspects of macroeconomics. The favourable responses to a questionnaire administered to students who used the programmed learning approach in the year 1971-72 have encouraged us to continue with this method of learning. The emphasis that instructors and students give to programmed learning in relation to lectures, tutorials, and the textbook will be completely determined by the individuals concerned. Presumably its merits will depend upon the degree of success that results from its use.

In this book we are interested in constructing a simple framework or "model" of the Canadian economy. Naturally, we do not claim that the model eventually developed is a true or even close representation of the Canadian economy. However, at an introductory level it is a useful first step in providing an analytical framework so that we may make some sense of concepts such as gross national product, unemployment, inflation, Canada's balance of payments, the foreign exchange rate, etc.

We would like to thank Ruth Paget and Joanne Fleming for typing the text, and our colleagues John N. Benson and Marion Steele for their most useful suggestions. Mary Reardon of Prentice-Hall provided excellent editorial assistance. All errors and omissions, however, are our responsibility.

D. A. L. A.
E. K. G.

CONTENTS

SUGGESTIONS FOR USING THIS BOOK

In this book you are required to complete sentences by writing the appropriate words, phrases, or numerical values in the blanks provided or crossing out the incorrect answers where choices are presented. By doing so, you will learn the key concepts and analytical techniques found in most introductory macroeconomics courses. We suggest that you try to complete each paragraph before checking your responses with the answers that appear at the bottom of the page.

MACROECONOMICS:

A PROGRAMMED BOOK FOR CANADIAN STUDENTS

ONE

MEASUREMENT OF NATIONAL OUTPUT

The Concept of National Output

1. The <u>value</u> of any single commodity (physical good) or service is its worth, and is usually expressed in terms of a price. As the value of a good or service increases, its ____________ is likely to rise. If there are several identical goods, the total money value would be the quantity times the price of each good. Total money value can change due to a change in ____________ or a change in ____________________ .

2. It is difficult to compare the values of different commodities (e.g., canoes and butter) simply by considering their physical quantities. However, money prices provide us with a common denominator or a standard unit of measure that allows us to compare the ____________ of different goods and services. In Canada, prices are expressed in terms of dollars.

3. Total value of an economy's output (national output) is determined by adding up the money values of all <u>final</u> (finished-state) goods and services produced in a given time period. For example, let us suppose that an economy produces butter, canoes, and doctors' services. In the following table the value of butter

---

1. *price; price, quantity (either order)*
2. *values*

produced is $ __________ , the value of canoes is $ __________ and the value of doctors' services is $ __________. The total value of national output in this example is $ ____________ .

Table 1-1

Good or Service	Quantity Produced	Price per Unit	Total Value of Output
Butter	5,000 lbs.	$1/lb.	
Canoes	100	$50/canoe	
Doctors' Services	500 hours	$4/hr.	

4. In the last paragraph we measured the total value of only final goods and services. A finished canoe is an example of a final good, and its value was $ ______ . Its production, however, requires approximately three stages: the manufacturing of cedar strips, the assembling of cedar strips into the basic hull, and the painting and finishing of the canoe. Let us suppose that the three stages were done by three different firms. Firm A manufactures the cedar stripping. The value of all the cedar stripping for one canoe sold to firm B, the assembler, is $25. This means that the (*price/value*) times the ______________ of the cedar strips was $25. This amount represents the cost of the lumber used plus the value of the manufacturing services of firm A to make the strips.

5. Firm B pays $ ______ for the cedar strips. After completing the hull, firm B sells the hull to firm C for $40 and in turn firm C

---

3. *5,000; 5,000; 2,000; 12,000*
4. *50; price; output*
5. *25*

pays $40 for the hull. Firm B then, added $ ______ to the value of the canoe.

6. After finishing the canoe, firm C sells it to the consumer for $50. Therefore firm C added $ ______ to the value of the canoe, and $50 represents the value of one finished canoe (a final good).

7. Notice in Table 1-2 that the value that has been added at each stage of production is $ ______ for stage one (firm A), $ ______ for stage two (firm B), and $ ______ for stage three (firm C), which equals $ ______ in total.

8. However, the selling prices at each stage were $ ______ when the canoe was sold by firm A to firm B, $ ______ when sold by B to C, and $ ______ when sold to the consumer. This totals $ ________ , which (*equals/does not equal*) the final value of $ ________ .

9. The summation of selling prices does not equal the value of the finished canoe. In Table 1-2 the summation of selling prices is $ ________. Notice that this money sum includes the contribution of firm A ____________ time(s). The money sum of firm B's contribution is included ____________ time(s), while firm C's contribution to production of the canoe is included ____________ . In contrast, the value of the finished canoe includes the contributions of each firm ____________ .

---

5. *15*
6. *10*
7. *25; 15; 10; 50*
8. *25; 40; 50; 115; does not equal; 50*
9. *115; three; two; once; once*

Table 1-2

Value of cedar strips (labour, profits, interest, rent) added by firm A	=	$25	
Selling price to firm B	=		$25
Value of cedar hull (firm B) sold to firm C	=		$40
Value added by firm B	=	$15	
Value of finished canoe sold to customer	=		$50
Value added by firm C	=	$10	

Value of one canoe = $50

10. If we were to use the money sum of selling prices at each stage we would clearly (*overstate/understate*) the value of the canoe. Hence, we would be in error if we used the selling price summation approach to estimate the value of the final product. We would be double counting the contributions of several firms, thereby (*overstating/understating*) the value of final output.

11. The production of one pound of butter possibly involves the stages shown below.

Table 1-3

Stages of Production	Selling Prices/lb.
milk production	30¢
butter production	50¢
packaging and distribution	70¢

Selling price to consumer = 70¢/lb. for final value

---

10. *overstate; overstating*

The value added by milk producers is ______ cents. The value added by butter producers is ______ cents, and the value added by the distributor is ______ cents. The value of a finished pound of butter is therefore ______ cents. The sum of selling prices is ________ cents and hence an overstatement of the value of the finished product.

12. We have emphasized that we wish to measure the value of final goods and services. Adding the value of all final goods and services produced in Canada gives us the value of national output at market prices in dollars (see Table 1-4). We stress the term market prices since goods and/or services that are not sold in markets are not included in the value of national output. For example, the services of housewives are not included because their services are not sold in a ______________ and so housewives receive no income.

13. However, if a householder hires and pays a housekeeper to do household duties, the value of the housekeeper's services (*will/will not*) be included in the value of national output.

14. Since volunteers offer their services free in such activities as political campaigns, United Appeal drives, etc., the value of their services (*will/will not*) be included in the value of national output.

---

11. *30; 20; 20; 70; 150*
12. *market*
13. *will*
14. *will not*

Table 1-4

Canada's National Output for the Last Five Years on a Yearly Basis

Year	Billions of Dollars
1966	61.4
1967	65.7
1968	71.4
1969	78.6
1970	84.5
1971	92.1

Source: Statistics Canada

Measurement of National Output in Canada

15. Statistics Canada in Ottawa collects data each year in order to measure the value of final goods and services. It does this in two ways. It collects data concerning the value of all purchases of goods and services in Canada. This is called the expenditure approach. In addition, it attempts to measure the income or payments received by all those persons who contribute to the production of goods and services sold in Canada. This is called the income approach. The two ways of measuring the value of final goods and services are the ____________________ approach and the ____________ approach.

16. The income approach measures total payments to owners of what are called factors of production. Factors of production include labour, land, capital (machines, factories, and other equipment), and entrepreneurship (organizational ability and financial risk). The owners of whichever factors of production are used to produce final output will receive ____________ payments.

---

15. *expenditure, income (either order)*
16. *income*

17. The owners of various factors of production receive specific income payments. Those who provide ______________ services receive <u>wages and salaries</u>. The owners of rented land and capital receive <u>rent</u> payments. <u>Interest</u> is paid to those who __________ money for investment in other factors of production. <u>Profit</u> represents ______________ payments to those who organize production and take financial risks.

18. In production of final output, capital becomes older and incurs wear and tear. The value of capital stock (*increases/declines*) in the course of production. This deterioration in the value of capital is called <u>depreciation</u>. Entrepreneurs will receive income (in this case from themselves) in the form of depreciation payments to cover the ____________________________ of their machines and other capital goods. It seems reasonable that the more intensively that capital is used, the (*higher/lower*) will be the ____________________________ payments to the owners of capital.

19. The canoe example in Table 1-2 will help us to understand the income approach. Specifically, we saw that value was added by firms A, B, and C. By producing cedar strips, firm A added $25 to the value of the canoe. Factors of production such as ______________, ______________, ______________, and ______________________________________ were required to produce cedar stripping. The owners of these factors of production received ______________ payments.

---

17. *labour; lend; income*
18. *declines; depreciation; higher; depreciation*
19. *capital, labour, land, entrepreneurship (any order); income*

20. Similarly, firm B added $15 to the value of the canoe, while firm C added $10. Income payments to owners of factors of production then, were $ ______ by firm B and $ ______ by firm C.

21. The value added by each firm represents the income payments of ________________ to lenders of money, ________ to owners of rented land and capital, ____________ to entrepreneurs, and ____________________________________ to workers.

Table 1-5

Expenditure and Income Arising from the Purchase or Production of One Canoe

Stage	Value Added by Firms	Payments to Persons	Expenditure for Purchase of Final Product
Cedar strips	$25	$25	
Constructing hull	15	15	
Finishing canoe	10	10	
	$50	$50	$50

22. Referring to Table 1-5, we see that total value added by the three firms is $ ______ , which is equal to the purchase price of the finished canoe. Since value added is equivalent to ____________ payments to the owners of factors of production, it follows that total payments to persons (*must equal/may differ from*) the purchase price of the finished canoe.

---

20. *15; 10*
21. *interest; rent; profit; wages and salaries*
22. *50; income; must equal*

23. Considering output for Canada as a whole (national output), the income approach must also yield the same result as the ______________________ approach. The term national output may be used interchangeably with national income or national expenditure. The measurement of national output at market prices by the income approach is known as gross national product (GNP). If national output is measured in terms of the value of purchases of final products, it is known as gross national expenditure (GNE). GNE is necessarily (*equal/not equal*) to GNP.

24. In Table 1-6 we list some of the major components of the income accounts for Canada in 1969. The largest component is ______________________________ .

Table 1-6

Canadian GNP in 1969 (billions of dollars)

Wages and salaries	43.2
Military pay	.9
Corporate profits before taxes;	7.9
deduct dividends paid to non-residents	- .8
Net income of unincorporated businesses	4.4
Net farm income	1.7
Interest and miscellaneous investment income	3.2
Inventory valuation adjustment	- .5
Net national income at factor cost	59.9
Indirect taxes less subsidies	10.6
Depreciation allowances	9.1
Error of estimate	- 1.0
GNP at market prices	78.6 *

* Components do not add up to total due to rounding.

Source: Statistics Canada

---

23. *expenditure; equal*
24. *wages and salaries*

25. In Table 1-7 we list the major components of the expenditure accounts for Canada in 1969. We will delay our discussion of the meaning of most of the components of GNE until Chapter 2. However, we draw to your attention the fact that ________________ expenditures are by far the largest component of GNE.

Table 1-7

Canadian GNE in 1969 (billions of dollars)

Consumption expenditures		46.5
Government expenditures		16.7
Total gross business investment		15.2 *
Plant and equipment	10.3	
Inventories	1.0	
Residential construction	3.8	
Net foreign trade (exports-imports)		- 1.0
Error of estimate		1.0
GNE		78.6*

* Components do not add up to total due to rounding.

Source: Statistics Canada

26. At this point, it might be helpful to define "gross" investment expenditures. Investment expenditures include outlays for factories, machines and other equipment, inventories (unsold goods), and residential construction. When a business firm purchases a new machine in order to expand its productive capacity, it has ________________ .

---

25. *consumption*
26. *invested*

27. It is important to realize that financial transactions are <u>not</u> included in the measurement of national income. Therefore, a takeover of one firm by another is <u>not</u> considered investment. It is merely a transfer of an asset. For example, if the Schlitz Brewing Company had successfully purchased Labatt Breweries of Canada, this purchase (*would/would not*) have been included in the GNE of that year. Similarly, if the Province of Ontario sells bonds to the general public, this does not appear in the national accounts because it is a financial transaction involving a

__________________ of an asset.

28. In each year, all capital deteriorates or depreciates slightly. Businesses allow for this depreciation by putting aside a sum of money that they feel represents the capital's depreciation. Thus if the total capital in an economy is $100 million and its depreciation is 10%, businesses will save $ ______ million for what is called <u>depreciation allowances</u>.

29. <u>Gross investment</u> includes depreciation allowances. When depreciation allowances are excluded from gross investment, the result is called <u>net investment</u>. For example, if gross investment were $100 million and depreciation allowances were $8 million, then net investment would be $ ______ million.

Net National Income and Expenditure

30. When the value of final output for the entire economy in terms of either income or expenditure is measured excluding depreciation

---

27. *would not; transfer*
28. *10*
29. *92*

allowances, the remaining value is known as the net national expenditure or the net national income. The net national income is equal to ________ minus ______________________________

______________________________ .

Personal Disposable Income

31. Another concept in national income analysis and one that is important for future analysis is personal disposable income. This is defined as the income payment received by individuals in the process of producing goods and services (GNP) plus transfer payments from the government (such as child allowances) minus what they pay out in the form of taxes. Thus, disposable income is defined as ________ minus _____________ plus ____________________ ____________________ . More specifically, if GNP is $100 million and taxes are $40 million and transfers are zero, then disposable income is $ ______ million.

Real vs. Money GNE

32. So far we have measured GNE in money values determined by money prices times (*quantity/expenditure*). Clearly, changes in prices and/or output will change the money value of GNE. Thus, if output remains unchanged and prices double, money GNE will ____________ . The doubling of money GNE (*would/would not*) indicate a doubling of output in physical terms.

---

30. *GNP; depreciation allowances*
31. *GNP; taxes; transfer payments; 60*
32. *quantity; double; would not*

33. Suppose that for two years the following information were given:

Table 1-8

Goods or Services	Year 1 (base year) Output (units)	Price/ Unit	Value	Year 2 Output (units)	Price/ Unit	Value
Canoes	100	$100	$10,000	100	$110	$11,000
Butter	5,000	1.00	5,000	5,000	1.10	5,500
Doctors' services	500	4.00	2,000	500	4.40	2,200
Total (Money) GNP			17,000			18,700
Total real GNP			17,000			17,000
Price index			100			110

In this example, money GNP has risen by $ ____________ or ______ %. The physical output of all goods and services has (*remained the same/risen*). Prices of all goods and services have (*risen/fallen*) by ______ %.

34. To determine whether or not physical output has changed from year 1 to year 2, it is necessary to adjust the money value of GNP in year 2 to take the price rise into account. This is done by deflating or dividing money GNP in year 2 by a price index. As an example, assume that year 1 is the base year. We see in Table 1-8 that the price index has gone from a base of 100 in year 1 to 110 in year 2. In order to get a deflated value of GNP in year 2, we must divide $ ______________ in year 2 by __________ . This

---

33. *1,700; 10; remained the same; risen; 10*
34. *18,700; 1.10*

will give us the value of output in year 2 in terms of prices in year 1. We call this real GNP. Since this value is (*equal to/greater than*) GNP for year 1 in our example, we can say that physical or real output (*has/has not*) changed.

Table 1-9

Goods or Services	Year 1 (base year) Output (units)	Price/ Unit	Value	Year 2 Output (units)	Price/ Unit	Value
Canoes	100	$100	$10,000	105	$105	11,025
Butter	5,000	1.00	5,000	5,250	1.05	5,512.50
Doctors' services	500	4.00	2,000	525	4.20	2,205
Money GNP			17,000			18,742.50
Real GNP			17,000			17,850
Price index			100			105

35. Money GNP has increased approximately 10% in the example shown in Table 1-9. Since prices of all goods and services have risen by ______ %, the increase in physical output (or real GNP) has been only ______ %. The real GNP in year 2 is calculated by dividing money GNP in year 2 by the price index, which in this case is ________ . Thus, real GNP in any year is determined by ________________ money GNP in that year by the ____________ ____________ for that year.

---

34. *equal to; has not*
35. *5; 5; 1.05; dividing; price index*

36. A decrease in real GNP is possible as well as an increase. For example, if money GNP rose 3% and prices of all goods and services rose by 5%, then real GNP would (*rise/fall*) by ______ % approximately. Or if money GNP went from \$100 million to \$105 million and the price index went from 100 to 110, then real GNP in year 2 would be \$ __________ million and indicate a (*rise/fall*) in real output between year 1 and year 2.

37. A comparison of money GNP for two years (*indicates/does not indicate*) whether real output has increased or decreased.

38. Since GNP can be measured either by the value of goods and services or by income payments, a fall in real GNP is equivalent to a (*rise/fall*) in real income, meaning that the economy has (*less/the same*) purchasing power.

39. Since the economic ability to purchase goods and services depends upon real income, then a fall in real GNP is equivalent to a (*rise/fall*) in the ability to purchase goods and services. If the real income of consumers fell, they would have (*less/more*) purchasing power.

40. If the ability to buy goods and services is one measure of economic well-being, then the economic well-being of society (*increases/decreases*) when real GNP falls. The change in money GNP, which (*indicates/does not indicate*) a decline or rise in real income, (*is/is not*) always an indicator of society's well-being.

---

36. *fall; 2; 95.5; fall*
37. *does not indicate*
38. *fall; less*
39. *fall; less*
40. *decreases; does not indicate; is not*

41. However, some price increases may reflect improvements in the quality of goods and services. A small rise in the price of a TV set may well be due to an improvement in reception. Notice that if your money income is fixed and you buy a TV at the increased price, you have less to spend on other goods and services than before the price increase. But this does not mean that your economic well-being has fallen, because the (*quality/price*) of one of your purchases has (*increased/decreased*). It is generally recognized that a 1-2% rise per year in the price level in Canada reflects quality changes.

42. The relevant price index that is used to ascertain real GNP is known as the GNP deflator, and this also is calculated by Statistics Canada through its data-gathering services. Figure 1-1 shows money GNP and real GNP for Canada for the years 1961 to 1969. Obviously, between 1961 and 1964 the GNP deflator (*was/was not*) rising as quickly as it was from 1965 to 1969.

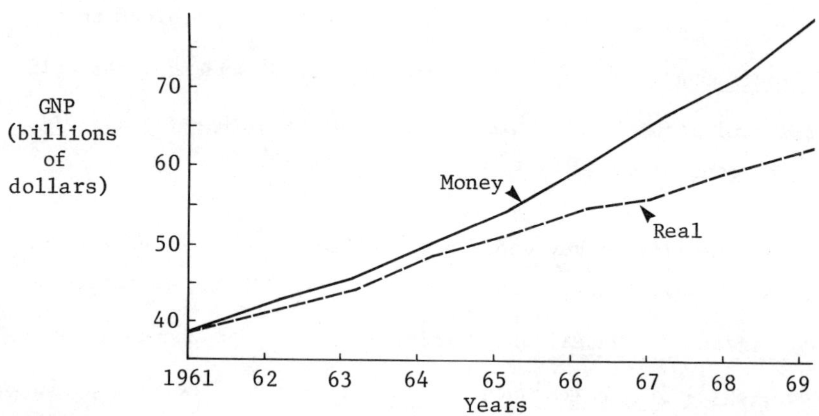

Source: Statistics Canada

Figure 1-1

---

41. *quality; increased*
42. *was not*

Potential GNP

43. As we have mentioned, Statistics Canada measures Canada's real GNP each year. We have also indicated that certain quantities of factors of production such as labour, land, and capital are required to produce a given real GNP. A given level of employment of labour is associated with a given level of GNP. We might draw up a hypothetical schedule of levels of real GNP and levels of employment:

Table 1-10

Real GNP	Employment of Labour
$30 billion	1 million
45	5
55	9
63	13

We notice that as more labour is employed, real GNP (*increases/ decreases*). With employment of 5 million workers, there would be a real GNP of $ ______ billion; a GNP of $63 billion is associated with an employment level of ______ million.

44. Let us suppose that 13 million represents the total labour force, which is defined as the number of persons over fourteen years of age who are willing to work in a given period of time. In Table 1-10, if the "actual" level of GNP is 63 billion, the number of employed workers is ______ million, which equals the ______________ ______________ ______________.

---

43. *increases; 45; 13*
44. *13; total labour force*

45. If the number of employed workers is equal to the size of the labour force, no unemployment of workers exists. According to Table 1-10, if the labour force consists of 13 million workers and actual GNP is $55 billion, the number of employed workers is ______ million and hence the number of unemployed workers is ______ million. In other words, the percentage of unemployed workers is approximately (*30/50/0*).

46. Full employment in this hypothetical example means that the number of employed workers equals the number in the labour force. However, at any given time in Canada approximately 3 1/2% of the labour force will be unemployed because various workers are changing jobs. Thus, most economists define full employment in Canada as 96 1/2% employment of the labour force. If at a given time 90% of the labour force is employed, then unemployment is said to be ______ %. Full employment is ______ % or less unemployed.

47. The level of real GNP corresponding to full employment is called potential GNP. Canada's potential real GNP is said to exist when (*96½ / 100*) % of the Canadian labour force is employed. Actual GNP is equal to potential GNP when only ______________ % of workers are unemployed. If more than 3 1/2% of workers are unemployed, actual real GNP is (*below/above/equal to*) potential real GNP. And if actual real GNP is less than potential GNP, resources are __________________________ . Many firms are not operating at capacity, or full utilization of available resources.

---

45. *9; 4; 30*
46. *6 1/2; 3 1/2*
47. *96 1/2; 3 1/2; below; unemployed*

This situation represents a loss in real ______________ and this is a cost to Canadian society. It seems desirable then, for economic policy to maintain __________ employment.

48. The following diagram from the Economic Council of Canada shows Canada's record from 1960 to 1969 and clearly indicates that full employment (*has/has not*) been achieved throughout this period.

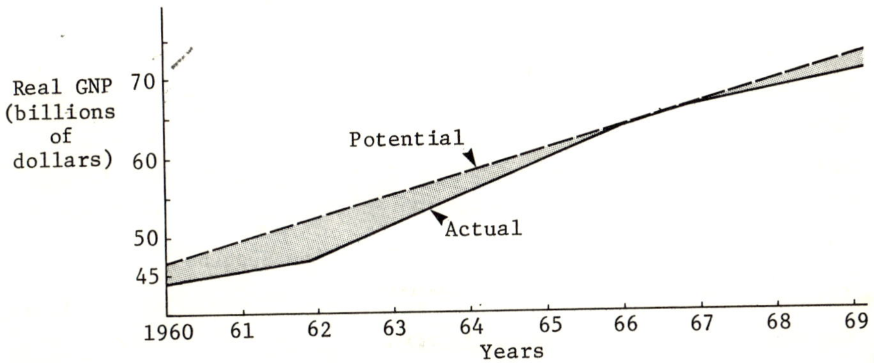

Source: Economic Council of Canada, Performance and Potential (Ottawa, 1970). Reproduced by permission of Information Canada.

Figure 1-2

---

47. *output; full*
48. *has not*

TWO

AGGREGATE DEMAND AND AGGREGATE SUPPLY

1. In this chapter we wish to establish a framework that allows us to distinguish between actual production and buying intentions in an economy in a given time period. The business community produces a certain money value of ____________ goods and services, based upon profit expectations, in a certain time period. This value represents actual production and is called aggregate supply.

2. From the last chapter we know that the value of national output of final goods and services is measured in two ways. For producing final goods and services, the owners of factors of production (labour, land, etc.) receive __________________ . Calculating national output by adding together these payments is called the income approach, and in this way we obtain the value for (GNP/GNE).

3. The other way of measuring national output is by aggregating the value of purchases of final goods and services. This is the __________________________ approach, and we obtain the value for (GNP/GNE).

4. Since the value of GNE is ____________ to the value of GNP, we may use these measurements interchangeably to denote the concept of aggregate supply. For convenience we shall use only GNP to denote aggregate supply.

---

1. *final*
2. *payments or income; GNP*
3. *expenditure; GNE*
4. *equal*

Equilibrium Levels of GNP

5. Aggregate supply, or _______ , is measured along the horizontal axis in Figure 2-1. As we move from left to right along this axis, the money value of aggregate supply (*increases/decreases*).

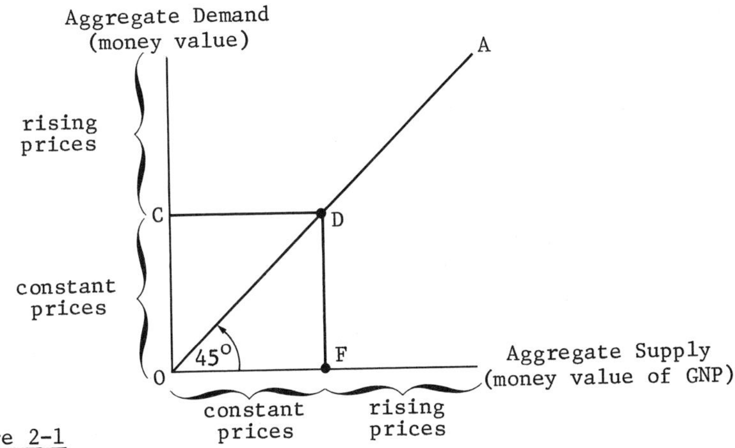

Figure 2-1

6. In the same time period, various decision makers (consumers, governments, business investors, foreign consumers, etc.) form intentions or plans to buy final goods and services. We call intended expenditures aggregate demand, and in Figure 2-1 this is measured on the vertical axis. When decision makers intend to spend more money to buy final goods and services, there is movement (*up/down*) the vertical axis.

---

5. GNP; *increases*
6. *up*

7. When buying intentions, which we called ______________________ ______________________, are equal to the <u>actual</u> money value of GNP, which we called ______________________ ______________________, an <u>equilibrium</u> exists. Simply stated, an equilibrium exists when buying intentions are exactly matched with actual production or GNP. Translating this back into formal terms, we say that when aggregate demand equals ______________________ ______________________ an ______________________ exists.

8. In Figure 2-1, any point on OA represents a condition where aggregate demand equals ______________________ ______________________, since OA is at a 45-degree angle to both axes. Point D represents a level of aggregate supply and aggregate demand where there exists full employment. Thus OF represents ______________ ______________________ GNP.

9. We assume that prices are constant between points O and F and between points O and C. Since prices are constant, there is no distinction between money and ____________ values for GNP and aggregate demand.

10. Prices are assumed constant between O and F because of the general tendency in the economy for prices to be rigid downward. When output falls (a movement from F toward O), businessmen tend to resist price cuts and labour unions to resist wage cuts. If this is the case, then when output falls to such a level that unemployment is generated, businessmen will ______________ price cuts and the general price level will tend to remain ______________________.

---

7. *aggregate demand; aggregate supply; aggregate supply; equilibrium*
8. *aggregate supply; full employment*
9. *real*
10. *resist; constant*

11. Similarly, increases in GNP between the ranges of 0 and F will tend not to generate price increases. Since any point to the left of F represents a situation of (*unemployment/full employment*), (*excess/insufficient*) capacity will exist for most firms. As a result, increases in prices will not be required to increase profits. The general price level will tend to be ____________.

12. On the other hand, since OF represents a maximum value of national output (at which resources are fully ________________) any increase in money GNP beyond point D must be due to a rise in (*prices/output*).

13. Similarly, since prices are assumed constant for money aggregate demand between 0 and C, money aggregate demand is equal to ________ aggregate demand. Beyond OD, prices are rising. If aggregate demand in Canada equals aggregate supply at full employment, prices (*are/are not*) constant and unemployment is __________ %.

14. We now introduce the notion of an aggregate demand line. It attempts to capture the idea that buying intentions (or ________________ ________________) are related to GNP. For reasons stated later, aggregate demand increases as GNP increases, and so the aggregate demand line has a (*negative/positive*) slope. If aggregate demand in Figure 2-2 were the line

---

11. *unemployment; excess; constant*
12. *employed; prices*
13. *real; are; 3 1/2*
14. *aggregate demand; positive*

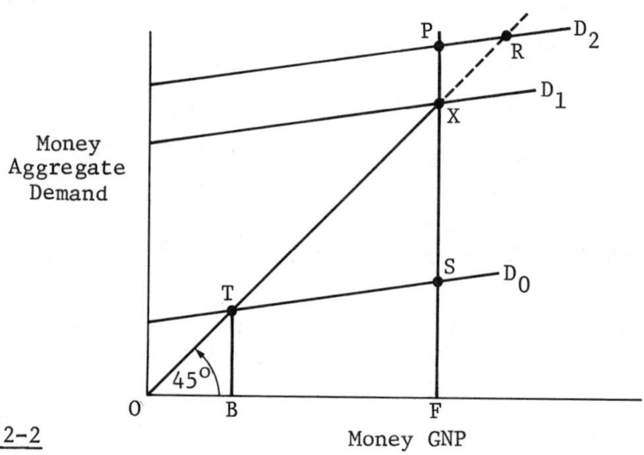

Figure 2-2

D_1, the economy would be in equilibrium at point X, a point where resources are fully ________________ . The level of potential GNP is represented by OF. If the aggregate demand line were D_0, equilibrium would be at point T, where GNP is at a level equal to (*OB/OT*). However, potential GNP is ______ , and at a GNP of OB, resources are ____________________ . Thus an economy may be at equilibrium, a situation where ____________________ ____________________ equals ____________________ ________________ , without having full ________________.

In order to obtain potential GNP and full employment, the aggregate demand schedule must be (*raised/lowered*). The distance between D_1 and D_0 (XS), at OF (potential GNP), is known as the recessionary gap. If D_0 coincided with D_1, there would exist no ____________________ resources.

---

14. *employed; OB; OF; unemployed; aggregate demand, aggregate supply (either order); employment; raised; unemployed*

15. If the aggregate demand schedule in Figure 2-2 were D_2, equilibrium would occur at point R. Since this represents a point beyond ______________ GNP, it follows that prices must (*increase/decrease*). This price inflation results from a level of aggregate demand that is more than sufficient to purchase the maximum output of the economy. As buyers compete for these scarce goods, the sellers react by (*decreasing/increasing*) their prices. In order to achieve a situation where there is no inflation, D_2 must coincide with ______ . The distance between D_2 and D_1 at potential GNP (XP) is called the inflationary gap. For the aggregate demand schedule D_1, there is no ______________ and no ______________ .

16. Let us now look at points on the aggregate demand curve that do not lie on OA. Such points represent situations in which buyers' intentions do not coincide with the amount of output, or the GNP. For example, we previously argued that at point T, aggregate demand equals ______________ ______________ , and so an equilibrium exists. At such a point, all buyers and suppliers are content with the existing conditions. However, at a point such as M in Figure 2-3, aggregate supply does not equal ______________ ______________ , and buyers and ______________ will adjust to restore an equilibrium situation. In a case like point M, aggregate demand is (*greater/less*) than aggregate supply since OV is greater than OW.

---

15. *potential; increase; increasing; D_1; inflation, unemployment (either order)*
16. *aggregate supply; aggregate demand; producers or suppliers; greater*

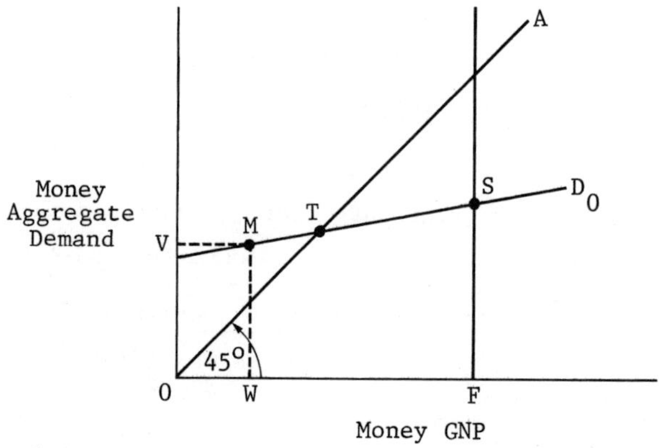

Figure 2-3

At this point, producers will find their stocks of goods (inventories) running down and will react by (*increasing/ decreasing*) production. They will change supply until aggregate supply is ______________________ aggregate demand, an equilibrium situation. For points like M then, the economy will react by (*increasing/decreasing*) real output.

17. Now consider a point like S. We can see that aggregate demand (*equals/does not equal*) aggregate supply. In fact, aggregate demand is (*greater/less*) than aggregate supply. In this situation, producers find that they have produced too much relative to aggregate demand, and they find the quantity of their unsold goods (*increasing/decreasing*). Hence, their inventories are

---

16. *increasing; equal to; increasing*
17. *does not equal; less; increasing*

accumulating unexpectedly. Suppliers are likely to react by (*increasing/decreasing*) their output, thereby reducing their needs for workers. If workers lose jobs, they are said to be ________________ . As workers are laid off, output and income (*rise/fall*) and there will be movement along the D_0 schedule until point ____ is reached, which represents an equilibrium.

18. Before we review the specific components of aggregate demand, it might be useful to distinguish between "autonomous" and "induced" expenditures. Induced expenditures are defined as those expenditures that depend on the level of national income or GNP. If GNP changes, induced expenditures ______________ . It is easy to see why these expenditures are called "induced"; a level of income induced a certain level of expenditures.

19. Autonomous expenditures are defined as those expenditures that do not depend on the level of GNP. If GNP changes, autonomous expenditures (*usually/do not necessarily*) change.

Components of Aggregate Demand

20. The largest component (in terms of value) of aggregate demand, as we have seen, is ________________________ expenditures. Household consumption expenditures have both autonomous and induced components. Consumption is influenced by real disposable

---

17. *decreasing; unemployed; fall; T*
18. *change*
19. *do not necessarily*
20. *consumption*

income. More specifically, the greater the level of real disposable income, the larger are consumption expenditures. If real disposable income falls, we would expect a (rise/fall) in consumption expenditures. Since taxes influence disposable income, a tax increase should cause disposable income to (rise/fall).

21. Generally speaking, disposable income depends upon the total income in the economy, so we can say that consumption expenditures are influenced by total income or by GNP. If GNP fell, we would expect consumption expenditures to (rise/fall). This relationship might be drawn as in Figure 2-4.

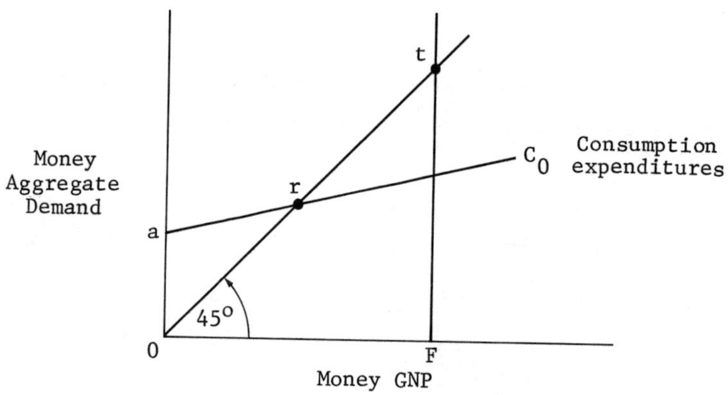

Figure 2-4

In Figure 2-4, OF represents potential income. Since prices are assumed constant between 0 and F, money income is equal to __________ income. We see from this diagram that as GNP

---

20. fall; fall
21. fall; real

increases, consumption expenditures (*increase/decrease*). The consumption function is (*upward/downward*) sloping.

22. Notice that at a GNP level of zero, consumption is equal to the distance ______ in Figure 2-4. This amount of consumption is known as autonomous consumption. We call it autonomous consumption because consumption may be determined by factors other than GNP. For example, consumer credit and past savings may allow consumers to spend, regardless of their current level of income. Autonomous consumption expenditures (*are/are not*) determined by the level of GNP.

23. However, from Figure 2-4 we can see that at any level of GNP greater than zero, the level of consumption expenditures is (*greater than/equal to*) Oa. This is so because consumption intentions are a function of GNP, and GNP is (*increasing/decreasing*) in a left-to-right direction in the diagram.

24. Table 2-1 shows hypothetical levels of consumption intentions and GNP for an economy. Such a schedule indicates one reason why we have represented aggregate demand as a line rather than a point; as GNP changes, consumption intentions change.

Table 2-1

C	GNP
$ 10 billion	$ 0 billion
50	50
90	100
130	150

---

21. *increase; upward*
22. *Oa; are not*
23. *greater than; increasing*

Since consumers intend to spend more because GNP has increased, these consumption plans are called ________________ expenditures. At a GNP level of zero, consumption is $ _____ billion. This we call ______________________ consumption. When GNP rises from zero to $50 billion, the (*rise/fall*) in consumption expenditures is $ _____ billion. Similarly, for each additional increment in GNP of $50 billion, consumption rises by increments of $ _____ billion. The ratio of the change in consumption to the change in GNP (symbolized by $\frac{\Delta C}{\Delta GNP}$) in Table 2-1 is (*1.0/0.8/0.9*) for each of the changes in GNP and consumption shown. This ratio is called the marginal propensity to consume, or the MPC.

25. We have drawn a diagram of the schedule given in Table 2-1.

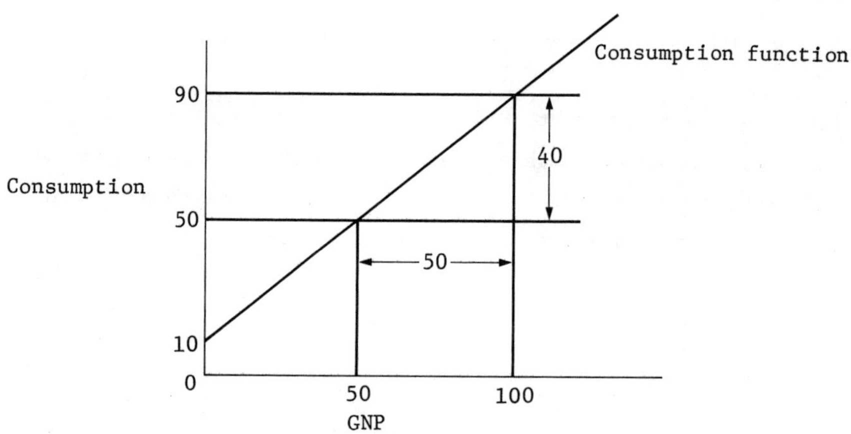

Figure 2-5

---

24. *induced; 10; autonomous; rise; 40; 40; 0.8*

In Figure 2-5, a change in GNP from \$50 billion to \$100 billion causes a (*rise/fall*) in consumption of \$ ______ billion. The MPC is $\frac{\Delta C}{\Delta GNP}$, which in this case is ______ . But notice that $\frac{\Delta C}{\Delta GNP}$ represents the slope of the consumption function. The ________ then, is the slope of the consumption function.

26. If the ratio $\frac{\Delta C}{\Delta GNP}$ is constant, we say that the ____________________ ________________________ to ____________________ is (*constant/changing*) and hence that the slope of the consumption function is (*constant/changing*).

27. The MPC is greater than zero and less than one. Thus the MPC is always (*positive/negative*). And, since the MPC is always (*positive/negative*), the slope of the consumption function is (*positive/negative*).

28. As we have seen, consumers spend a certain proportion of their income. The remaining proportion is called <u>savings</u>. Total income minus consumption is called ____________________ . If an individual's income is \$8000 and he spends \$7200 on consumption goods, his savings is \$ (*8,000/800/7,200*).

29. We previously showed a hypothetical schedule of levels of consumption and GNP. It is now possible to compute the level of savings for each level of GNP. In Table 2-2, savings is equal to \$ ________ billion at a level of GNP of \$150 billion.

---

25. *rise; 40; 0.8; MPC*
26. *marginal propensity; consume; constant; constant*
27. *positive; positive; positive*
28. *savings; 800*
29. *20*

Table 2-2

GNP	Consumption	Savings
$ 0 billion	$ 10 billion	$ -10 billion
50	50	0
100	90	10
150	130	

30. If there were only consumption expenditures in an economy, aggregate demand would equal ______________________ . This is shown in Figure 2-6.

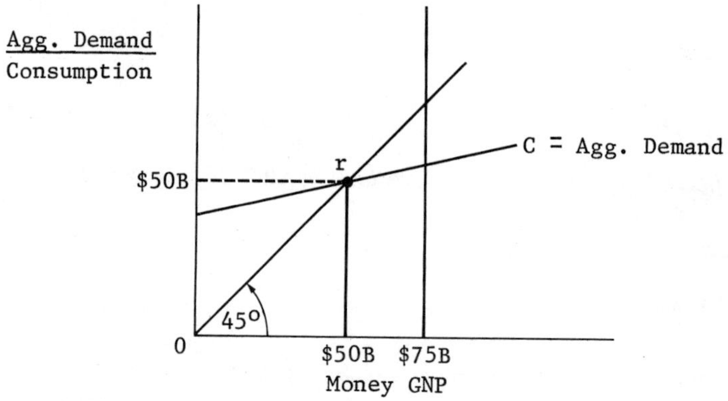

Figure 2-6

The aggregate demand curve is upward sloping because the MPC is (*positive/negative*) or the slope of the consumption function is (*positive/negative*). For such an economy, the equilibrium level of GNP is $ ______ billion, where ____________________ ____________________ equals aggregate demand. However, $50 billion does not necessarily represent full employment.

---

30. *consumption; positive; positive; 50; aggregate supply*

31. Investment, or business expenditure on plant, equipment, and inventories, is another component of ______________________ demand. There are a number of factors that influence the business decision to make investment expenditures. For example, the businessman compares the expected rate of return of an investment project with the cost of borrowing. If the rate of return is greater than the cost of borrowing (interest rate), the businessman will invest. If the interest rate is reduced, investment expenditures are likely to (*increase/decrease*). Thus investment expenditure is partly determined by the ______________________ ______________ .

32. Expectations, that is, what the businessman thinks will happen to profits in the future, also affect investment. If expectations are such that a strong growing economy is foreseen for the future, the businessman is more likely to proceed with capital expenditures in order to expand the capacity of his business. If expectations are for unemployment and recession, investment expenditures are likely to be (*reduced/expanded*). Thus, two factors that influence investment expenditures are the ________________ ______________ and ___________________________ .

33. Assuming that investment expenditures do not depend on the level of GNP but on the interest rate and the state of expectations, then investment expenditures are said to be autonomous. The line I_0 in Figure 2-7 indicates that businessmen intend to spend OI_0,

---

31. *aggregate; increase; interest rate*
32. *reduced; interest rate; expectations*

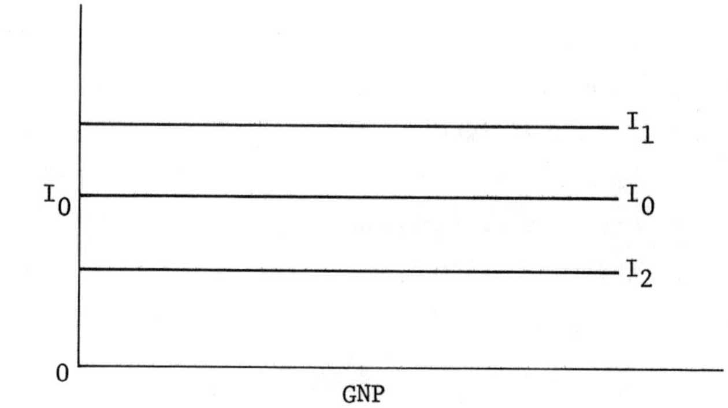

Figure 2-7

based on the current interest rate and state of expectations, at every level of GNP. Investment intentions are (*constant/ not constant*) for every level of ________ and therefore are ________________________.

34. When expectations and/or the rate of interest change, the level of investment changes. A shift from I_o to I_1 might result if there were a (*rise/fall*) in the interest rate or if businessmen became more ________________________ about profit expectations. Conversely, the investment line would shift ____________________ if the interest rate rose and businessmen became ____________________ about future profits.

---

33. *constant; GNP; autonomous*
34. *fall; optimistic; downward; pessimistic*

35. In a hypothetical world without government, aggregate demand is now composed of ______________________________ plus ______________________________. These are shown in Figure 2-8 as C_0 and I_0.

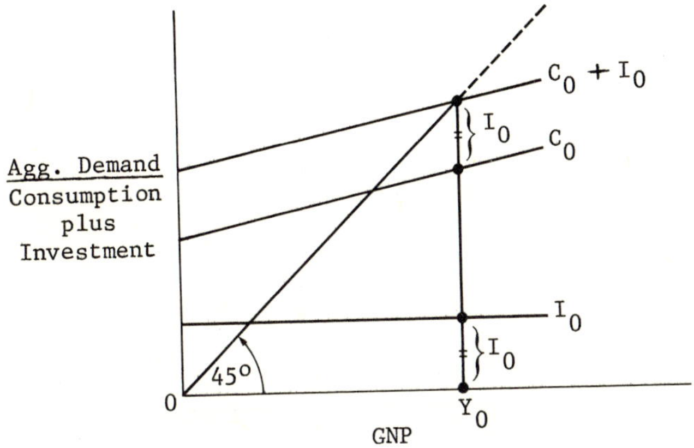

Figure 2-8

If we add vertically I_0 to C_0, the aggregate demand curve becomes $C_0 + I_0$. The difference between $(C_0 + I_0)$ and C_0 at any level of gross national product is the difference between the horizontal axis and I_0.

36. If the interest rate declines, I_0 in Figure 2-8 will likely shift (*upward/downward*) and the aggregate demand curve will shift (*upward/downward*). The new equilibrium level of GNP will be (*greater/less*) than Y_0.

---

35. *consumption, investment*
36. *upward; upward; greater*

37. Let us now add government expenditures to our model of the economy. The level of such expenditures, like investment, is determined by a number of factors. We assume that these expenditures do not depend on the level of GNP and so they are said to be

________________________. If factors are constant for a given time period, government expenditures may be shown by the curve in Figure 2-9.

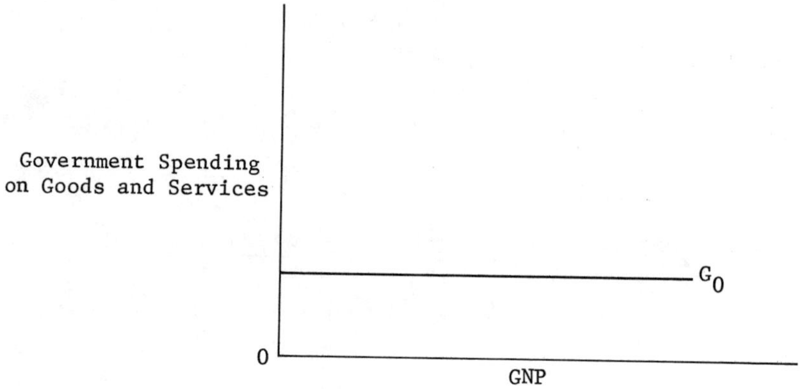

Figure 2-9

If government decides to spend more money on defence, the government expenditure curve will shift (*upward/downward*). If there is a reduction in expenditure on highways and schools, the curve will shift (*upward/downward*).

38. If we add autonomous investment and autonomous government expenditures to consumption, aggregate demand becomes C + I + G and is shown in Figure 2-10.

---

37. *autonomous; upward; downward*

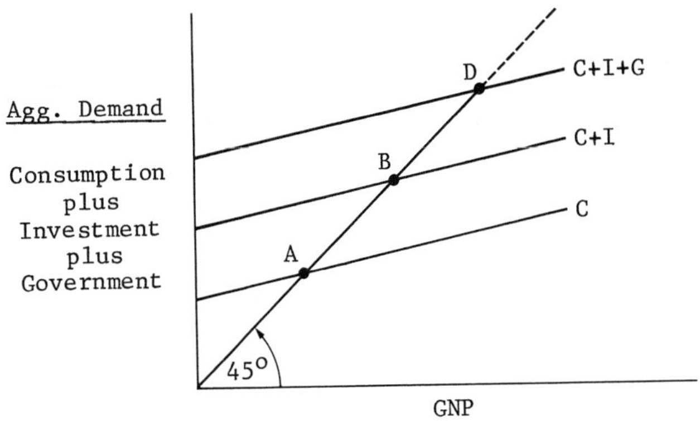

Figure 2-10

The vertical distance between the C and the C + I curve is ________________ expenditures, and the vertical distance between the C + I and the C + I + G curve is ________________ expenditures. In this example, the equilibrium level of gross national product at point D is potential GNP and so resources are ________ ____________.

39. Canada is very much involved in trading with other countries. Goods sold to foreign countries are exports, and goods purchased from other countries by Canadians are imports. Exports are a component of aggregate demand because they are goods produced in Canada and provide employment and income for Canadians. Imports, on the other hand, are subtracted from aggregate demand, since they represent the substitute of foreign goods for Canadian goods and so the income goes to foreigners rather than to Canadians.

If Canada buys more U.S. automobiles, (*imports/exports*) will

---

38. *investment; government; fully employed*
39. *imports*

(*decline/rise*) and if the Chinese buy more Canadian wheat, (*imports/exports*) will (*decline/rise*). Since exports and imports are determined by many factors, including the economic policies of other countries, we might represent them by Figure 2-11.

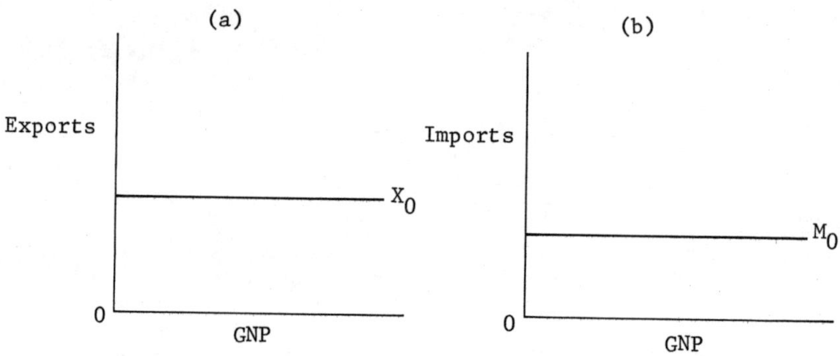

Figure 2-11

As depicted in the diagrams, both import and export expenditures are assumed to be (*autonomous/induced*).

40. Adding exports to aggregate demand and subtracting imports from aggregate demand produces the following aggregate demand schedule for the Canadian economy. In Figure 2-12, C + I + G + (X - M) represents the total aggregate demand for the economy. If exports increased, the aggregate demand curve would shift (*upward/downward*). If investment declined, the aggregate demand curve would shift (*upward/downward*). If government expenditures increased by $5 million and investment decreased by $5 million, aggregate demand would (*increase/decrease/remain the same*).

---

39. *rise; exports; rise; autonomous*
40. *upward; downward; remain the same*

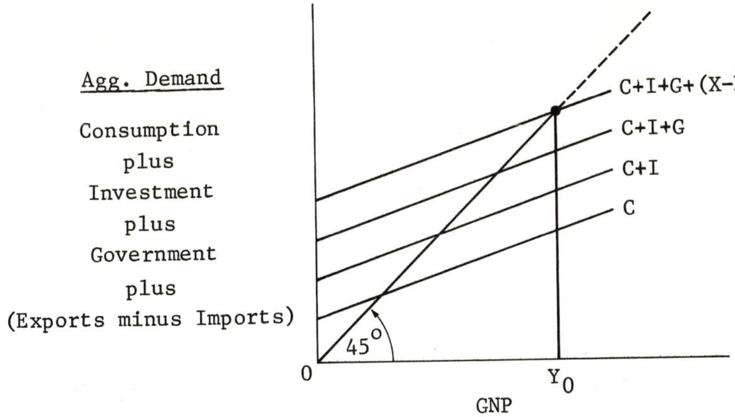

Figure 2-12

41. If aggregate demand and the equilibrium level of gross national product is shown as Y_o, and Y_o represents potential income in Figure 2-12, then resources in the economy are ______________ ______________. An increase in aggregate demand to beyond Y_o would result in a (*rise/fall*) in the price level.

42. Equilibrium GNP is achieved at a point where ______________ ______________ is equal to ______________ ______________. If this equilibrium level is below potential GNP, there will be ______________ resources at equilibrium. Inflation will occur when aggregate demand is above the level necessary to ensure that the economy reaches ______________ GNP.

---

41. *fully employed; rise*
42. *aggregate demand, aggregate supply (either order); unemployed; potential*

THREE

MULTIPLIER ANALYSIS

1. Recall from the previous section that prices are assumed (*constant/falling*) for levels of gross national product below potential GNP. For all levels above potential GNP, it is assumed that the price level is (*constant/rising*).

2. Since prices are unchanged for levels of gross national product below potential GNP, we concentrate our attention on the effect of changes in aggregate demand on real output. To review, the components of aggregate demand are ______________________________ , ______________________________ , ______________________________ , and ______________________________ .

3. Figure 3-1 shows an aggregate demand schedule of D_1. Gross national product is at an equilibrium level at Y_o, and Y_1 is potential GNP. At Y_o there are ______________________________ resources in the economy. Notice that a movement from W to S along D_1 will not result in an equilibrium level of potential GNP, because at S aggregate demand does not equal ______________________________ ______________________________ .

---

1. *constant; rising*
2. *consumption, investment, government, exports minus imports (any order)*
3. *unemployed; aggregate supply*

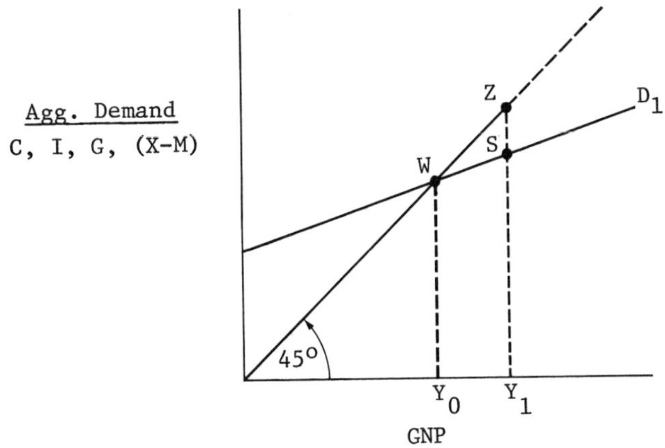

Figure 3-1

4. To achieve an equilibrium at Y_1, it will be necessary to shift the aggregate demand curve (*upward/downward*) so that it crosses the aggregate supply curve at point ____ .

5. The shift in aggregate demand necessary to reach Y_1 at equilibrium is equal to (*WS/SZ*). This vertical distance we call the recessionary gap or what other authors have called the deflationary gap. The recessionary gap is equal to the difference between aggregate demand at potential GNP and a given level of aggregate demand below potential GNP.

6. In order to achieve potential GNP when there are unemployed resources in an economy, there must be a change in aggregate demand equal to the ______________________ gap.

7. Suppose for the moment that consumption is the only component of aggregate demand. We depict a consumption function in Figure 3-2.

---

4. *upward; Z*
5. *SZ*
6. *recessionary*

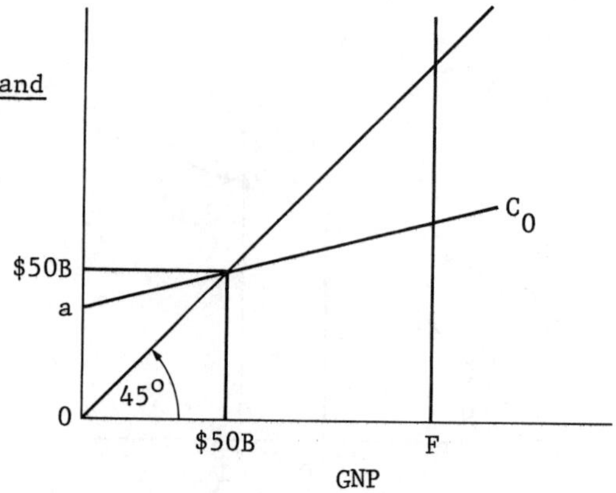

Figure 3-2

We stated earlier that at a GNP level of zero, consumption would be given by the distance ______ ; this we call ____________________ consumption. The slope of the consumption schedule is equal to the ____________________ ________________________ to ____________ and is (*constant/changing*) in Figure 3-2.

8. The equilibrium level of GNP in Figure 3-2 is $ ______ billion. If OF represents potential GNP, a level of $50 billion for GNP represents a situation where there are (*unemployed/fully employed*) resources.

9. Now let us suppose that at each level of GNP (including zero), consumers decide to spend $5 billion more than is shown by Oa. This would be illustrated by a(n) (*upward/downward*) shift in the consumption curve.

---

7. *Oa; autonomous; marginal propensity; consume; constant*
8. *50; unemployed*
9. *upward*

10. The new consumption curve along with the old consumption curve is shown in Figure 3-3.

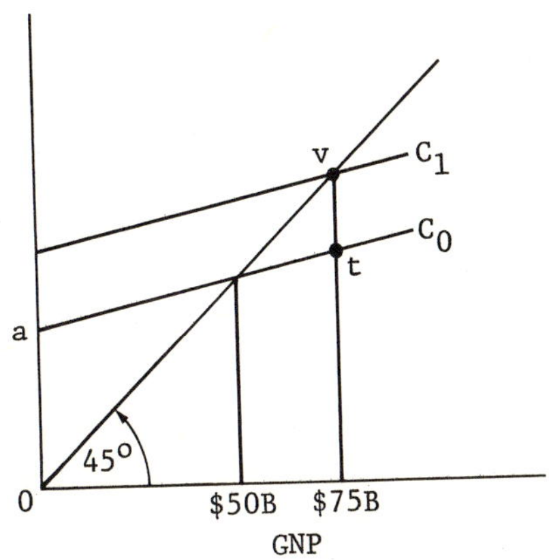

Figure 3-3

The new equilibrium for gross national product is $ _______ billion. The distance tv equals $ (*5/25*) billion, which is the change in autonomous ______________________________ expenditures.

11. The change in the equilibrium level of gross national product is equal to $ ______ billion. From Figure 3-3 it can be seen that this change in gross national product, given by the distance 50-75, is (*greater than/equal to*) the change in autonomous consumption, which is equal to $ ______ billion. The change in gross national product is obviously a multiple of the change in autonomous consumption. This fact is the basis for the multiplier analysis.

12. Let us look at how the change in GNP is a multiple of the change in autonomous consumption. The first change in GNP is the in-

---

10. *75; 5; consumption*
11. *25; greater than; 5*

crement in autonomous consumption of $ ______ billion. This is shown in Figure 3-3 by the distance tv, which is equal to an increase of $ ______ billion in aggregate demand. The increase in consumption represents the purchase of final goods and services. The producers and sellers of these goods and services will receive payment (or income) of $ ______ billion. We know from previous discussion that an increase in income will lead to a further increase in ____________________________ .

13. If the marginal propensity to consume is 0.8, then a change in income of $5 billion will result in a change in consumption of $ ______ billion. Since consumption is a component of aggregate demand, ______________________ __________________ will increase by $4 billion. This latter change in consumption is equal to the value of the marginal propensity to consume times the change in income (MPC x ΔY). Accordingly, savings have increased by $ ______ billion.

14. So far the change in GNP (ΔY) is equal to the change in autonomous consumption, which was $ _______ billion, plus the resulting change in consumption, which was $ _______ billion, for a total of $ _______ billion.

15. The process continues. There will be a second round of consumption expenditures since the additional $4 billion in new consumption expenditures will become $4 billion of new income to other

---

12. *5; 5; 5; consumption*
13. *4; aggregate demand; 1*
14. *5; 4; 9*

individuals. If the MPC is 0.8, they will spend $ _______ billion on consumption goods out of their additional income of $ ________ billion. Given that consumption has risen by another $3.2 billion, then _________ has risen by the same amount.

16. As of this point, ΔY is equal to the initial change in consumption plus the first round's increase in consumption plus the second round's increase in consumption. This sum is $ ________ billion.

17. This process will continue for many rounds until gross national product reaches a new equilibrium of $75 billion. If the original level of GNP was $50 billion, the increase in gross national product has been $ ______ billion. The ratio of ΔY to the initial change in autonomous expenditures is ______ . This is the numerical value of what has been called the multiplier.

18. Fortunately, the multiplier is given by a simple expression: $\frac{1}{1-MPC}$. Because the MPC is the only variable in this expression, we can say that the numerical value of the multiplier depends on the numerical value of the ________ .

19. In the above example the MPC was 0.8. Substituting 0.8 for MPC, our multiplier formula yields one divided by (*0.8/0.2/5*), which is equal to a value of (*5/0.8/1.25*).

---

15. *3.2; 4; GNP*
16. *12.2*
17. *25; 5*
18. *MPC*
19. *0.2; 5*

20. In summary, it is relatively easy to ascertain the final effect on GNP of a change in autonomous consumption by using the multiplier analysis. For our example, a $5 billion change in autonomous consumption caused a final change in GNP of $ ______ billion. This is denoted symbolically as $\Delta Y = \frac{1}{1\text{-MPC}} \times \Delta C$. The multiplier is the $\frac{1}{1\text{-MPC}}$ term and, with an MPC of 0.8, has a value of (*0.8/5/1*). The change in autonomous consumption, ΔC, was $5 billion, and by the above formula, ΔY should be $ (*25/5/0.8*) billion.

21. We have stated that the value of the multiplier depends on the MPC. If the MPC were 0.9, the multiplier would be (*0.1/10/1.1*); if the MPC were 0.75, the multiplier would be (*1.3/4/5*). Notice therefore that as the MPC increases, the value of the multiplier (*increases/decreases*).

22. If ΔC increased by $5 billion and the MPC were 0.75, the final value of ΔY would be $ (*3.75/15/20*) billion; if the MPC were 0.9, ΔY would be $ (*6/50/4.5*) billion.

23. Let us suppose that instead of increasing, autonomous consumption declines by an amount of $5 billion. This will result in a(n) (*upward/downward*) shift in the consumption curve, and the new equilibrium level of GNP will be (*below/above*) the original level. If the MPC is 0.5, the multiplier will be ______ and the change in gross national product will be $ ______ billion.

---

20. *25; 5; 25*
21. *10; 4; increases*
22. *20; 50*
23. *downward; below; 2; -10*

24. Another component of aggregate demand is investment expenditure. Suppose that the expectation of profits and sales becomes more optimistic. This is likely to cause a (*rise/fall*) in investment and shift the investment curve in a vertical direction. The aggregate demand curve will shift (*upward/downward*) by the amount of the increase in investment. This is shown in Figure 3-4.

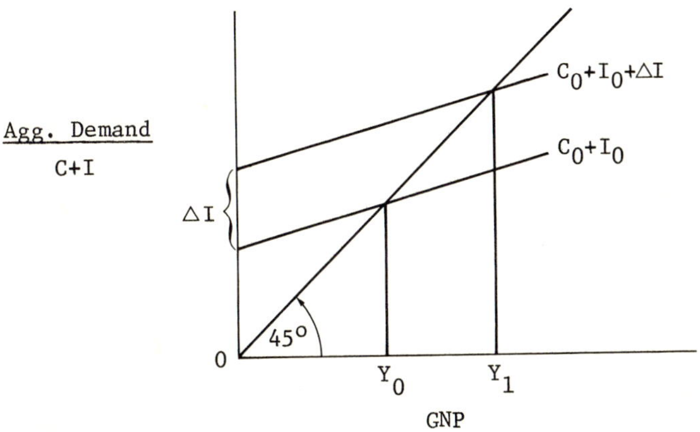

Figure 3-4

25. The equilibrium level of gross national product in Figure 3-4 has increased from the distance ______ to ______ , and we see that again the change in gross national product appears diagrammatically to be (*greater/less*) than the change in investment. The change in gross national product is a multiple of the change in investment. The process that generates this multiplier effect has been explained above for a change in autonomous consumption and is the same for autonomous investment. If the marginal propensity to consume is 0.8 and the increase in investment is $20 billion, the final change in gross national product is $ ________ billion.

---

24. *rise; upward*
25. *Y_0; Y_1; greater; 100*

26. A third component of aggregate demand is government expenditures. The effect of changes in this component on gross national product will be discussed in detail in the chapter on fiscal policy.

27. The first item of the fourth component of aggregate demand is exports to other countries from Canada. Suppose China decides to buy less wheat from Canada. This will result in a (*fall/rise*) in Canadian exports. The aggregate demand will shift (*upward/downward*), and Canadian GNP will fall. This is shown in Figure 3-5, where gross national product has changed from the distance ______ to ______ .

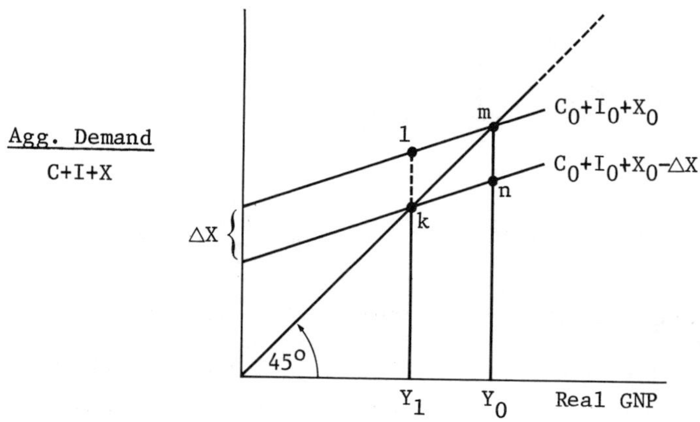

Figure 3-5

The aggregate demand curve has shifted vertically by the change in exports, which is shown by $-\Delta X$ (i.e., $lk = mn = -X$).

28. Using the multiplier process described above, and assuming that exports fall by \$6 billion and the marginal propensity to consume

---

27. *fall; downward;* Y_0*;* Y_1

is 0.75, the total fall in gross national product is $ ______ billion. If instead, the marginal propensity to consume were 0.5 and exports declined by $6 billion, the total fall in GNP would be $ ______ billion.

29. Thus, positive changes in components of aggregate demand produce positive multiple changes in gross national product, whereas negative changes in aggregate demand cause ____________________ ____________________ changes in gross national product.

30. The second item of the fourth component of aggregate demand is imports, or purchases by Canadians of goods from other countries. A rise in imports caused by a shift of Canadian preferences to foreign goods means less spent on the Canadian output of consumer goods and less income for Canadians. The effect on GNP is similar to the effect of foreigners' deciding to buy fewer Canadian-produced goods. A rise in imports is likely to lead to a (*decline/rise*) in Canadian GNP; likewise a decline in exports leads to a (*decline/rise*) in Canadian GNP.

31. As in changes in other components of aggregate demand, a change in imports will have a multiplier effect on gross national product. A (*decline/increase*) in imports will lead to a fall in GNP, whereas a fall in imports will lead to a (*rise/fall*) in GNP.

32. The amount by which gross national product will change is determined by the multiplier mechanism described above for other

---

28. *24; 12*
29. *negative multiple*
30. *decline; decline*
31. *increase; rise*

components of aggregate demand. If the marginal propensity to consume is 0.9 and there is an increase in imports of $2 billion, GNP will finally (*rise/fall*) by $ ______ billion.

33. In summary then, we have seen that when one or more components of aggregate demand change, there will be changes in GNP (*equal to/greater than*) these changes in aggregate demand. The amount of the change in GNP depends crucially on the ____________________ ____________________ to ______________, from which one can estimate the value of the ____________________.

34. Having developed the value of the multiplier, we may now compute values of recessionary and inflationary gaps more precisely than before. In Figure 3-6, $100 billion represents the full employment level of income, and the aggregate demand schedule is represented by D_0D_0. We have depicted a (*recessionary/inflationary*) situation. However, the economy is at an equilibrium level of GNP of $ ______ billion.

35. In order to restore full employment, GNP must be increased by $ ______ billion. From Figure 3-6 we see that the aggregate demand line must be shifted (*upward/downward*) by the distance (*sv/st/tv*).

36. It is possible to calculate the magnitude of the recessionary gap if we know the value of the multiplier. The numerical value of the gap is equal to the value of the change in GNP necessary to

---

32. *fall; 20*
33. *greater than; marginal propensity; consume; multiplier*
34. *recessionary; 60*
35. *40; upward; sv*

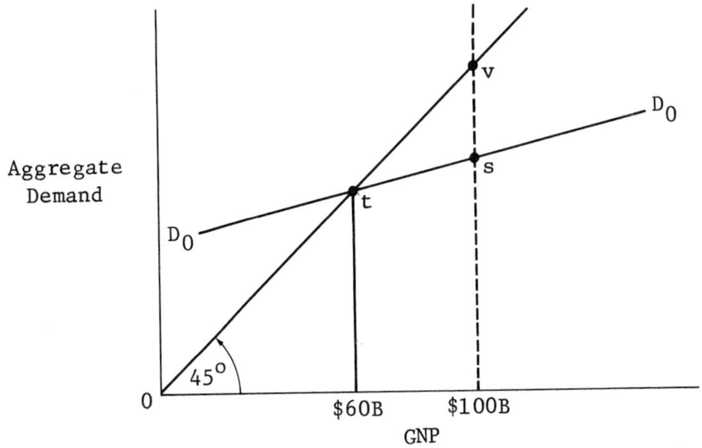

Figure 3-6

obtain full employment, divided by the value of the multiplier. If the MPC were 0.75, the value of the multiplier would be ______ . In the previous example, GNP must rise by $ ______ billion to restore full employment. Therefore the numerical value of the recessionary gap is $ *(10/133/40)* billion.

37. The above example illustrates that aggregate demand must change by an amount *(equal to/greater than)* the value of the recessionary gap to restore full employment.

38. The preceding method can be used to compute numerical values of inflationary gaps as well. If full employment with stable prices is given as $100 billion but the GNP is $150 billion, then a(n) ______________ gap exists. The needed change in the money value of GNP to restore full employment with constant prices is $ ______ billion. If the multiplier had the value of 10, the gap would be $ ______ billion.

---

36. *4; 40; 10*
37. *equal to*
38. *inflationary; 50; 5*

39. Thus, aggregate demand must (*increase/decrease*) by an amount (*equal to/greater than*) the value of the inflationary gap to achieve a constant price level.

40. Chapter 4 deals with ways in which various levels of government in Canada deal with recessionary and inflationary gaps. Clearly, government expenditures and taxes affect ______________________ ________________ and may be used to solve problems of inflation and recession.

NOTE: Students interested in more complicated models of the economy will find them in the Appendix.

---

39. *decrease; equal to*
40. *aggregate demand*

FOUR

FISCAL POLICY

1. It will be recalled that the desired state of the economy is one in which there is full ______________ and price increases of less than *(1-2/10/20)* % per year. Unfortunately this is not always the situation. At times, aggregate demand may be equal to aggregate supply at less than full employment GNP and there will then be a ______________ gap. Or aggregate demand may exceed aggregate supply at full employment, in which case there will be ______________ .

2. If there were unemployment, full employment could be attained only if the aggregate demand schedule were shifted *(upward/downward)*. If there were inflation, price stability would require a(n) *(upward/downward)* shift in the aggregate demand schedule.

3. We have seen that one component of ______________ ______________ is government expenditures on goods and services. Since the government can decide to increase or decrease expenditures, it can ______________ or ______________ aggregate demand.

4. We have also seen that government revenue (taxes) is subtracted from personal income to obtain personal ______________

---

1. *employment; 1-2; recessionary; inflation*
2. *upward; downward*
3. *aggregate demand; increase, decrease (either order)*
4. *disposable*

income. A reduction in taxes would (*increase/decrease*) disposable income, and a rise in taxes would (*increase/decrease*) disposable income. If consumption expenditures depend upon disposable income, an increase in taxes would (*increase/decrease*) consumption expenditures; a lowering of taxes would (*increase/decrease*) consumption expenditures. Changes in taxation could influence expenditures and so change ________________ ______________ . Altering taxes or government expenditures to affect aggregate demand is known as fiscal policy.

5. If the economy were suffering from unemployment, the government could (*increase/decrease*) its expenditures on goods and services and thus shift the aggregate demand schedule (*upward/downward*). Such a change is illustrated in Figure 4-1, where aggregate demand has increased from D_o to D_1.

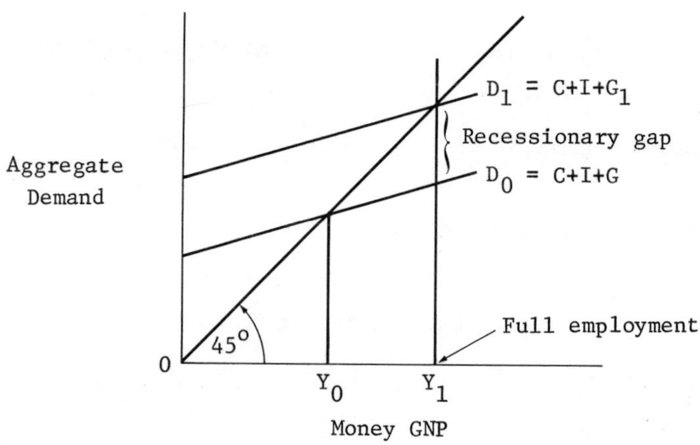

Figure 4-1

4. *increase; decrease; decrease; increase; aggregate demand*
5. *increase; upward*

6. As a result of government policy to increase expenditures on goods and services, gross national product in Figure 4-1 increases from ______ to ______ . Since prices in this range of gross national product are assumed (*constant/rising*), the rise in money GNP or national income equals the rise in _________ GNP or real national income. At Y_1 there is full ______________________ .

Government Expenditure Multiplier

7. The rise in real GNP is (*greater/less*) than the increase in government expenditures, due to the operation of the multiplier. If the increase in government expenditures were $100 million and the multiplier were 3, money and real GNP would rise by $ ________ million.

8. Government expenditures can also be used to reduce inflationary pressures. In Figure 4-2, the aggregate demand schedule D_o illustrates that aggregate demand is (*greater/less*) than aggregate supply at full employment, so ______________ are rising. If the government were to reduce its expenditures by an amount equal to st, the level of aggregate demand would (*rise/fall*) to D_1, and the (*inflationary/recessionary*) gap equal to the distance ______ would be eliminated. If government expenditures were reduced by more than the distance st, a situation of (*unemployed/fully employed*) resources would follow.

---

6. *Y_0; Y_1; constant; real; employment*
7. *greater; 300*
8. *greater; prices; fall; inflationary; st; unemployed*

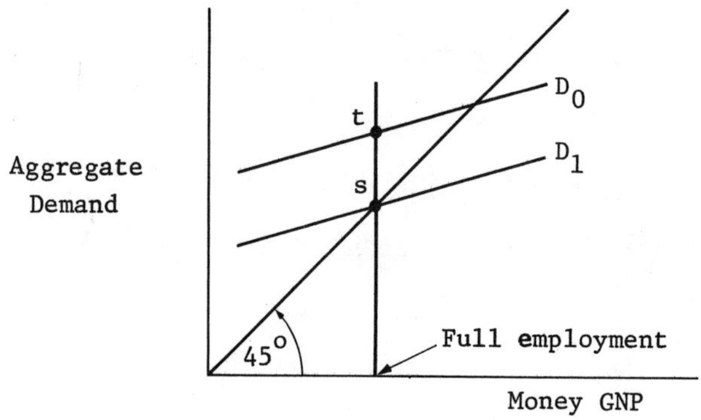

Figure 4-2

9. In addition to changing expenditures on goods and services, the government might also change ____________ to reduce the level of aggregate demand and control ____________________ . Or tax changes could be used to raise aggregate demand and hence reduce ___________________________ . Since income taxes affect disposable income and thus consumption expenditures, we shall have to examine the (*consumption/government*) component of aggregate demand when analyzing the effects of taxes.

Tax Multiplier

10. A tax reduction of $10 million means that disposable income will (*increase/decrease*) by $ ______ million. If the marginal propensity to consume out of disposable income is 0.8, then consumption will increase by $ ______ million and savings will increase by $ ______ million. The consumption schedule will shift upward by

---

9. *taxes; inflation; unemployment; consumption*
10. *increase; 10; 8; 2*

$ ______ million. Whenever income taxes are lowered, the consumption schedule will shift by an amount equal to the amount of the tax change times the ________ .

11. If taxes are increased, the consumption schedule will shift (*upward/downward*) by an amount equal to the rise in ____________ times the ________ .

12. Since a change in taxes affects the consumption schedule, a change in taxes also affects the aggregate demand schedule. If taxes are reduced, the consumption schedule shifts (*upward/downward*) and the aggregate demand schedule shifts (*upward/downward*).

13. As a result of an upward shift in the consumption and aggregate demand schedules, gross national product will (*increase/decrease*) by an amount equal to the change in consumption times the ________________________ . Since the change in consumption is equal to the change in tax times the MPC, it follows that the change in GNP due to a tax reduction is equal to (the change in taxes) x (MPC) x (the multiplier)

or

$$(\Delta T) \times (MPC) \times \frac{1}{1 - MPC}$$

which equals

$$(\Delta T) \times \frac{MPC}{1 - MPC}$$

14. If government expenditures had been changed, the increase in gross national product would be equal to the change in government

---

10. *8;* MPC
11. *downward; taxes;* MPC
12. *upward; upward*
13. *increase; multiplier*

expenditures times $\frac{1}{1 - MPC}$. Thus the multiplier associated with a tax change is *(greater/less)* than the multiplier associated with an expenditure change.

15. If the MPC is equal to 0.8, a tax reduction of \$100 million will result in an expansion of gross national product equal to \$ ______ million. The fraction $\frac{MPC}{1 - MPC}$ is known as the tax multiplier and is always *(greater/less)* than the expenditure multiplier by *(one/two/three)*.

16. Figure 4-3 illustrates the use of a tax cut to stimulate aggregate demand and achieve full employment. The line D_2 represents a schedule of aggregate demand that is *(greater/less)* than aggregate supply at potential GNP, and hence a level where there are

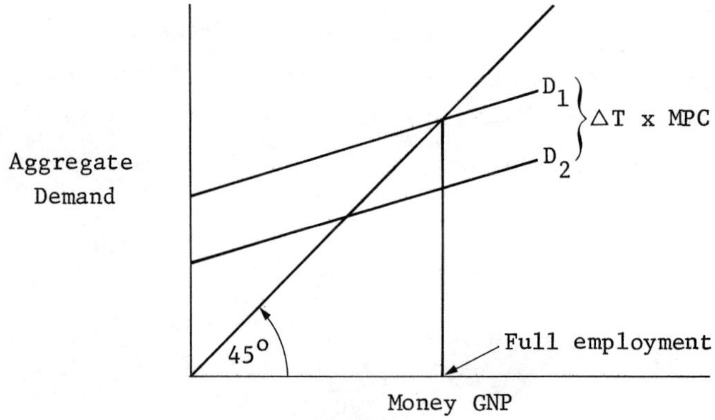

Figure 4-3

---

14. *less*
15. *400; less; one*
16. *less*

_______________ resources. When taxes are reduced and disposable income increased, (*consumption/government*) expenditures increase and the aggregate demand schedule becomes D_1, where there is no _______________.

17. If the tax cut were $200 million and the MPC equal to 0.75, the consumption schedule would shift upward vertically by the amount of the tax cut times the ________.

18. Using the tax multiplier, the rise in GNP would be the (*increase/decrease*) in taxes times the multiplier, or $ (600/200/100) million.

19. In addition to changing government expenditures on goods and services, and taxation, the government could increase or decrease transfer payments such as unemployment benefits and welfare cheques. An increase in such payments would likely (*increase/decrease*) consumption expenditures, and the level of _______________ _______________ would (*increase/decrease*). Increases in transfer payments have the same effect on aggregate demand as tax (*increases/decreases*), while reductions in transfer payments are similar to tax (*increases/decreases*).

Combined Changes in Taxes and Expenditures

20. So far we have dealt with changes either in expenditures or in taxation. The government may wish to change both of these

---

16. *unemployed; consumption; unemployment*
17. MPC
18. *decrease;* 600
19. *increase; aggregate demand; increase; decreases; increases*

simultaneously. Suppose the economy is suffering from unemployment, a situation that calls for a ____________________ in taxation and a (*rise/decline*) in government expenditures.

21. If the MPC is 0.75, a tax reduction of $2 billion will __________ GNP by $ _____ billion. A rise in expenditures of $3 billion will __________________ GNP by $ _____ billion. The total __________________ in GNP will therefore be $ _____ billion.

22. A rise in government spending of $3 billion will, as we saw above, raise GNP by $ _____ billion, but an increase in taxes of $2 billion will (*increase/decrease*) GNP by $ _____ billion. In this case the net impact on GNP will be a (*rise/decline*) of $ _____ billion.

23. It is interesting to ascertain the effect on GNP if the government were to increase expenditures by the same amount as it increases taxes. This we call a balanced budget policy because government expenditures are then equal to government revenue, which consists of (*tax/transfer*) proceeds.

24. Let us suppose that the government raised its expenditures by $10 million. If the MPC were equal to 0.8, then the multiplier is _____ and the final (*increase/decrease*) in GNP would be $ _____ million.

---

20. *reduction; rise*
21. *increase; 6; increase; 12; increase; 18*
22. *12; decrease; 6; rise; 6*
23. *tax*
24. *5; increase; 50*

25. If the government also increases taxes by $10 million and the MPC is 0.8, then the tax multiplier is _____ and the final (*increase/decrease*) in GNP from the tax change is $ ______ million.

26. The combined changes in GNP in paragraphs 24 and 25 give us the net effect of a balanced budget policy on GNP. The effect has been to (*increase/decrease*) GNP by $ ______ million.

27. The final change in GNP expressed as a ratio of the change in government expenditures is (*10/1/0*). This ratio is called the balanced budget multiplier.

28. If government expenditures were equal to revenue and the government only increases its expenditures or only reduces taxes, this would produce a level of expenditures (*greater/less*) than the amount of tax revenues. This situation is known as a government budget deficit and is likely to occur when the government is trying to raise ____________________ ____________________ and increase the (*employment/prices*) of resources.

29. A budget surplus would be a situation in which (*expenditures/taxes*) exceed (*expenditures/taxes*) and might occur during an inflationary period in which the government (*increases/decreases*) taxes to reduce aggregate demand.

30. Since the government has special powers such as taxation and creation of money, there is generally nothing preventing the

---

25. *4; decrease; 40*
26. *increase; 10*
27. *1*
28. *greater; aggregate demand; employment*
29. *taxes; expenditures; increases*

government from having a budget deficit as a means of achieving __________ employment GNP.

31. In summary then, during a recession we would generally expect fiscal policies such as (*increases/decreases*) in taxes and (*increases/decreases*) in ______________________________, possibly resulting in a budget (*surplus/deficit*). In a period of inflation, the appropriate fiscal policy would be a(n) (*increase/decrease*) in expenditures and/or (*increase/decrease*) in taxes, with a possible budget surplus.

---

30. *full*
31. *decreases; increases; expenditures; deficit; decrease; increase*

FIVE

MONEY AND THE CANADIAN BANKING SYSTEM

1. Transactions involved in the purchase and selling of goods and services may be conducted in many ways. One method is simply a barter system of exchange. For example, a transaction might be conducted between two individuals such that so many oranges are exchanged for so many apples. A system of exchange that involves exchanging a quantity of goods for another quantity of goods is called a ______________ system.

2. A barter system is cumbersome and inefficient. Modern economies have therefore developed monetary systems to facilitate transactions. The two significant characteristics of money are general acceptability and convenience. For an article to become money, it must be generally ________________ and ____________________ to use.

3. One component of the money supply in Canada consists of coinage produced by the Canadian Mint and paper notes issued by the Bank of Canada, the country's central bank. Coins and Bank of Canada notes are generally ________________ and ____________________ and so are used as money.

4. However, coins and notes constitute only about one-fourth of Canada's money supply. The other three-fourths consists of

---

1. *barter*
2. *accepted; convenient*
3. *accepted; convenient*

chequable deposits in the chartered banks of Canada. Canada's money supply then, consists of ____________ and ______________ ______________________________ and ________________________ ______________ in the chartered banks.

5. People find chequable bank deposits very convenient. They may write cheques, based on the money in their accounts, to conduct large transactions; their money is protected while they are not using it; and often they receive interest payments on their deposits from the chartered banks. In addition, cheques are generally accepted in Canada. So bank deposits have the positive characteristics of money. And given that deposits have several attributes that make them preferable to currency, it is no wonder that chequable bank deposits represent the (*major/minor*) component of Canada's money supply.

6. It is important to realize that only the existence of a deposit in a bank allows an individual to write a cheque. The ability to write a cheque is assumed by the existence of a ______________. When a cheque is written by individual A and accepted by individual B, the bank deposit of individual A (*increases/decreases*) by the amount of the cheque. Bank deposits represent assets to depositors. Therefore, when people write cheques, their assets of bank deposits (*increase/decrease*).

7. Not all deposits in banks can be used for chequing purposes. Any deposits that are not chequable deposits (*are/are not*) considered as money.

---

4. *coins, Bank of Canada notes (either order); chequable deposits*
5. *major*
6. *deposit; decreases; decrease*
7. *are not*

8. Chequable deposits held in a chartered bank are liabilities for the bank, since the bank must pay out currency when cheques are drawn on these accounts or people withdraw money from their accounts. When a cheque is cashed, a bank's liabilities (*increase/decrease*). When a person deposits money in a bank, the bank's liabilities (*increase/decrease*).

9. Banks in Canada encourage people to hold deposits, because the banks use this money to make loans that yield profits. After all, banks are businesses and, like other businesses, are concerned with profits. The more loans they extend, the greater the ________________ they make.

10. One of the major assets that a bank holds is loans to individuals and businesses. Bank loans are assets to the bank, since the borrowers must pay both principal and interest to the bank. Banks make money by ________________ money to ______________________ and ________________________ . However, loans represent liabilities to individuals and businesses. Bank loans then, are (*assets/liabilities*) to the bank and (*assets/liabilities*) to individuals and businesses.

11. If a bank could loan out all of its deposits, the value of its loan assets would equal the value of its __________________ .

12. However, in Canada banks are not allowed to lend out all of their deposits. They are required by law to hold a certain amount of their deposits as what are called reserves. The value of a bank's

---

8. *decrease; increase*
9. *profits*
10. *lending; individuals, businesses (either order); assets; liabilities*
11. *deposits*

deposits then, (*equals/does not equal*) the value of the bank's loans. In fact, the value of bank loans is (*greater/less*) than the value of the bank's deposits.

13. Reserves consist of cash held in the bank (or vault cash) and chartered bank deposits at the Bank of Canada. The latter is the major component of reserves. Just as an individual may have a deposit in a chartered bank, chartered banks may have deposits in Canada's central bank, the Bank of Canada. Reserves are the (*cash/liabilities*) held by the chartered bank, and its (*deposits/loans*) at the Bank of Canada.

14. As we have mentioned, chartered banks by law must hold a certain quantity of reserves. These are called required reserves. More specifically, banks are required to hold a certain ratio of their total deposits in the form of reserves. This ratio is known as cash reserve ratio (CRR). For example, if a bank is required to hold \$10 million in reserves and has deposits of \$100 million, the CRR is equal to ______ %. Or, if the CRR is 8% and a bank has \$125 million in deposits, it is required to hold \$ ______ million in reserves.

15. A simplified balance sheet (sometimes called a T-account) for a chartered bank is shown in Table 5-1.

Table 5-1

Assets		Liabilities	
Cash reserves	\$ 40M	Deposits	\$200M
Loans	160M		
	\$200M		\$200M

---

12. *does not equal; less*
13. *cash; deposits*
14. *10; 10*

If this bank is holding the minimum required cash reserves, the CRR must be ______ %. Loans and cash make up the bank's ____________, and deposits form its __________________________ .

Expansion and Contraction of Deposits

16. When a bank receives a new deposit of $10 million, deposits increase by $10 million and cash reserves increase by $10 million. If the CRR is 10% the portion of the deposit that the bank must hold as cash (or its <u>required cash reserves</u>) is $ ______ million and the remaining $ ______ million may be loaned to the public. Following a new deposit, the difference between <u>actual</u> cash reserves and <u>required</u> cash reserves is <u>excess cash reserves</u> and is the amount available for _____________ .

17. Balance sheets for banks A, B, and C are shown in Table 5-2, where the CRR for all is 10%. If deposits increase in bank A by $10 million, cash reserves would have to increase by at least $ ______ million and the <u>excess</u> cash reserves of $9 million could be used for _____________ . But loans can only be made if the bank is willing to lend and people are willing to ______________ .

18. Let us suppose that after the new deposit in bank A, the bank loaned the $9 million to one customer. This customer buys $9 million worth of lumber from a lumber company, which accepts a cheque from the buyer and deposits it in bank B. As a result, deposits would increase in B by $ ______ million. The minimum

---

15. *20; assets; liabilities*
16. *1; 9; loans*
17. *1; loans; borrow*
18. *9*

Table 5-2

A

Assets		Liabilities	
Cash	$ 15M	Deposits	$150M
Loans	135M		
	$150M		$150M

B

Assets		Liabilities	
Cash	$10M	Deposits	$100M
Loans	90M		
	$100M		$100M

C

Assets		Liabilities	
Cash	$ 20M	Deposits	$200M
Loans	180M		
	$200M		$200M

increase in B's cash reserves would be $ ______ million, and loans could increase by $ ______ million.

19. Finally, suppose that bank B loaned this amount to a customer who deposits the cheque in bank C. Deposits in C would increase by $ ______ million, while the increase in its minimum cash reserves would be $ ______ million. Loans could then rise by $ ______ million.

20. As a consequence of one initial deposit of $10 million, deposits in the three banks have increased by $10M + $9M + $8.1M = $27.1 million, while loans have risen by $9M + $8.1M + $7.29M = $24.39 million. Cash reserves have increased by $ __________ million.

21. If such an expansion of deposits (or of the money supply) were to go on and on in the same way, the increase in deposits would eventually be $100 million, with a possible increase in loans of $90 million. The minimum increase in cash reserves would be

---

18. *0.9; 8.1*
19. *8.1; 0.8; 7.29*
20. *2.71*

$ ________ million. The increase in deposits is equal to D_1 divided by CRR, where D_1 is the initial change in deposits. If the CRR were 25% an initial increase of $50 million in deposits in a bank could lead to an ultimate expansion in deposits of $ ________ million. Loans could then (*increase/decrease*) by $ ________ million.

22. The preceding examples dealt with the expansion of bank deposits. When there is an initial decline in deposits, the following occurs:

Table 5-3

Initial Position (CRR = 10%)

Assets		Liabilities
Cash	$ 50M	Deposits $500M
Loans	450M	

After Withdrawal

Assets		Liabilities
Cash	$ 50M	Deposits $500M
	-10M	-10M
	$ 40M	
Loans	$450M	
	$490M	$490M

Deposits now decline by $10 million because someone makes a withdrawal from the bank by writing a cheque on their account. Deposits and of course cash fall by $10 million. Now $40 million is not 10% of $490 million. In fact, the bank must add $ ______ million to its cash reserves. This is done by calling in $9 million that individuals and businesses have borrowed, as outlined in Table 5-3(a). The bank is able to do this because it has some of its loans out on a day-to-day basis with no fixed time limit.

---

21. *10; 200; increase; 150*
22. *9*

Table 5-3 (a)

Step 2

Assets				Liabilities	
Cash		$ 40M		Deposits	$490M
	+	9M	$ 49M		
Loans		$450M			
	-	9M	441M		
			$490M		

23. With a CRR of 20%, loans in a single bank will (*increase/decline*) by $ ________ million if deposits decline by $50 million.

24. Just as the principle of multiple deposit expansion applies when deposits initially increase, an initial decline in deposits will lead to a multiple (*expansion/contraction*) of deposits and loans in the banking system.

25. The final possible reduction in deposits and loans will depend upon the size of the CRR. If the CRR is 10% and the initial decline in deposits is $10 million, the ultimate (*expansion/contraction*) of deposits is $ ________ million.

26. If the cash reserves remained at their legal level, loans would be reduced by $ ________ million. Since the change in reserves must equal the difference between the change in deposits and the change in loans, reserves must decline by $ ________ million.

27. So far we have shown that changes in deposits can affect the amount of loans made by the banks. A change in the CRR can also accom-

---

23. *decline; 40*
24. *contraction*
25. *contraction; 100*
26. *90; 10*

plish this end, but such a technique is not at present allowed in Canada by the Bank Act. For analytic purposes, however, suppose that the CRR rises from 10 to 20% from one period to the next. Show how this affects the balance sheet by filling in the blanks in Table 5-4.

Table 5-4

Period 1 (CRR = 10%)

Assets		Liabilities
Cash	(a) $ ______ M	Deposits $100M
Loans	(b) $ ______ M	

Period 2 (CRR = 20%)

Assets		Liabilities
Cash	(c) $ ______ M	Deposits $100M
Loans	(d) $ ______ M	

28. Thus a (*rise/fall*) in the CRR would increase the amount of loans the banking system can make.

Interest, Loans, and the Money Supply

29. In order to obtain a loan from a bank, a borrower must agree to pay interest on the amount borrowed. The proportion of the amount borrowed that must be paid as interest is the rate of interest.

The cost of borrowing money then, is called ____________________ .

30. When the interest rate is high, individuals and businesses will not be as eager to borrow money as when the interest rate is low. If the interest rate is lowered, bank loans will tend to (*increase/decrease*).

---

27. (a) 10; (b) 90; (c) 20; (d) 80
28. *fall*
29. *interest*
30. *increase*

31. Banks try to loan out all their deposits over and above what they must hold as cash reserves. If no one wants to borrow, the banks could (*raise/lower*) the ____________ ____________ to encourage borrowing.

32. When there are many people who want to buy few goods, the goods are said to be scarce and their prices will (*rise/fall*). Similarly, when there is a limited supply of money for loans and people want to borrow, the rate of interest will (*rise/fall*).

33. Since deposits are an important determinant of the money available for loans, and deposits form a large part of the money supply, changes in the ____________ ____________ can affect the availability of loans.

34. A decrease in deposits (part of the money supply) will likely (*increase/decrease*) loans and (*increase/decrease*) interest rates.

---

31. *lower; interest rate*
32. *rise; rise*
33. *money supply*
34. *decrease; increase*

SIX

THE BANK OF CANADA AND MONETARY POLICY

1. When the government of Canada requires cash over and above the cash it receives from taxes, it may sell bonds to the public (individuals and businesses) and to chartered banks. A government bond is simply a financial contract whereby a member of the public or a chartered bank agrees to lend the government a sum of money, for example $1,000. The government agrees to return this sum plus interest, perhaps 5% ($50), at the end of some time period, for example one year. Thus, if government spending exceeds tax revenue, one way of raising funds is for the government to __________ bonds to the ______________ and ______________________ ______________ .

2. The Bank of Canada, Canada's central bank, acts as an agent of the government. It is <u>not</u> part of the system of chartered banks. The central bank holds the government's bonds (those not held by the public or chartered banks) as <u>assets</u>. If the Bank of Canada sells bonds to the public, the ______________ of the Bank of Canada (*increase/decline*).

3. In Chapter 5, we saw that the cash reserves of a chartered bank form part of the bank's assets. Although they are clearly assets to the chartered bank, it is required by law that most of these reserves be held in a deposit account with the Bank of Canada.

---

1. *sell; public; chartered banks*
2. *assets; decline*

Personal deposits show up as liabilities in a chartered bank.

Thus, cash reserves show up as (*assets/liabilities*) in the Bank of Canada. The Bank of Canada is not required to hold reserves. A very simplified balance sheet (T-account) for the Bank of Canada might show:

Table 6-1

Bank of Canada

Assets	Liabilities
Government of Canada bonds	Deposits of chartered banks (Reserves)
	Bank of Canada paper notes

4. We have said (paragraph 1) that the chartered banks may buy government bonds. Bonds are another form of asset for the chartered banks since they are redeemable for cash. Assets of chartered banks are thus composed of cash reserves, loans, and

________________ ________________ . A simple balance sheet (T-account) of a chartered bank might be:

Table 6-2

Assets		Liabilities	
Cash	$ 10M	Deposits	$100M
Loans	80M		
Government bonds	10M		
	$100M		$100M

---

3. *liabilities*
4. *government bonds*

Open Market Operations

5. Let us now see what happens when the Bank of Canada sells a $10 million government bond to a member of the public. If the purchaser presents a cheque to the Bank of Canada for the bonds, the purchaser's ________________ in a chartered bank (*decline/expand*). The cash reserves of the chartered bank (*decline/expand*) by the same amount. Because reserves are held as deposits in the Bank of Canada, there is a decline in the (*assets/liabilities*) of the central bank. Since the central bank gives the bonds to the purchaser, the ________________ of the central bank (*decline/expand*). The dollar value change in the assets of the Bank of Canada is matched by the dollar value change in its liabilities. As a result, the accounts of the Bank of Canada balance.

Table 6-4

Bank of Canada

Assets	Liabilities
Canadian government bonds - fall	Reserves of chartered banks - fall

Public

Assets	Liabilities
Canadian government bonds - increase	
Public deposits in chartered banks - fall	

---

5. *deposits; decline; decline; liabilities; assets; decline*

Table 6-4 (Cont.)

Chartered Bank

Assets	Liabilities
Reserves in Bank of Canada - fall	Public's deposits - fall

6. Suppose the Bank of Canada buys $15 million worth of bonds from an individual who places this money in his deposit account at a chartered bank. Show the initial changes in the balance sheets of the central bank, the individual, and the chartered bank where the individual has a deposit account.

(a) Bank of Canada		(b) Chartered Bank		(c) Individual	
Assets	Liabilities	Assets	Liabilities	Assets	Liabilities

7. We have already seen that a chartered bank may hold government bonds as part of its assets. Suppose the initial position of a chartered bank were:

Table 6-5

(CRR = 10%)

Assets		Liabilities
Cash reserves	$ 100M	Deposits $1,000M
Loans	800M	
Government bonds	100M	
	$1,000M	

If this bank purchases $10 million worth of bonds from the central bank, the chartered bank's cash reserves will (*expand/decline*) by

---

6. (a) *Assets*: *Government Bonds + $15M; Liabilities: Reserves of Chartered Banks + $15M*
(b) *Assets*: *Reserves + $15; Liabilities: Deposits + $15M*
(c) *Assets*: *Government Bonds - $15M; Deposits in Chartered Banks + $15M*

7. *decline*

$ ______ million and its holdings of government bonds will increase by $ ______ million. In order to maintain a minimum legal CRR of 10%, loans would initially have to be (*increased/reduced*) by $ ______ million to meet the cash reserve requirement.

8. The operations in paragraphs 5, 6, and 7 dealt only with the initial effect of bond purchases or sales. In Chapter 5, we showed that initial changes in deposits can lead to multiple contraction or expansion of the ______________ ______________ . Since by ______________ or ______________ government bonds from or to the public and chartered banks the Bank of Canada can change deposits and/or reserves of chartered banks, it can control the money supply.

9. At any given moment, government bonds are held by individuals, businesses, chartered banks, and the Bank of Canada. If the Bank of Canada wanted to expand the money supply it would __________ bonds, and if it were selling bonds it would be trying to (*expand/contract*) the money supply. Such operations to expand or contract the money supply by buying or selling bonds are known as open market operations.

10. Suppose the economy were suffering from inflation as a result of aggregate ______________ exceeding full employment aggregate ______________ . One possible reason for this is the existence of too much money in the economy. The Bank of Canada could

---

7. *10; 10; reduced; 10*
8. *money supply; buying, selling (either order)*
9. *buy; contract*
10. *demand; supply*

____________________ the supply of money by __________________ government bonds to the public and chartered banks. Such ________ _______________ operations are known as <u>restrictive monetary policy</u>.

11. In paragraph 7, the Bank of Canada was dealing with a chartered bank. In that case, existing chartered bank deposits were not initially affected. Now consider a case where the Bank of Canada deals with a corporation that has a deposit account in a chartered bank. Suppose the Bank of Canada sold $10 million of bonds to General Motors of Canada, which paid for them with a cheque drawn on its account at the Bank of Montreal. Deposits of the Bank of Montreal would (*increase/decline*) as would its ______________ ____________________ . If the cash reserves prior to the bond transactions were equal to the minimum legal requirement and the CRR were 10%, the Bank of Montreal would have to ______________ its loans by $ ________ million to maintain the minimum cash reserves required by law.

12. Applying the principle of multiple contraction of bank deposits and loans, the policy in paragraph 11 would lead eventually to a decline in bank deposits of $ ________ million and a decline in loans of $ ________ million.

13. The balance sheet for a chartered bank is shown in Table 6-6.

---

10. *reduce; selling; open market*
11. *decline; cash reserves; reduce; 9*
12. *100; 90*

Table 6-6

(CRR = 10%)

Assets		Liabilities	
Cash	$ 20M	Deposits	$100M
Loans	80M		
	$100M		

Suppose that the Bank of Canada sells $10 million in bonds to Molson's Brewery, which pays for these by cheque drawn on the above bank. After the bond transaction, the bank's cash reserves are $ ______ million and deposits are $ ______ million. Actual cash reserves (*exceed/equal*) the minimum requirement. The loans of this bank (*would/would not*) have to be reduced as a result of this restrictive policy. On the assets side of the central bank's balance sheet, ______________ ______________ would (*increase/decline*) by $10 million, and on the liabilities, ______________ would (*increase/decline*) by $ ______ million.

14. The example in paragraph 13 indicates that the success of restrictive open market operations may be reduced when actual cash reserves (*exceed/equal*) the minimum legal requirements.

15. In summary then, ideal conditions for a multiple contraction of deposits (money supply) due to open market operations require that all of the following hold true: (a) actual reserves of the chartered banks are initially (*equal to/greater than*) the required legal reserves; (b) the chartered banks and public are willing to (*buy/sell*) bonds from/to the Bank of Canada; (c) chartered bank

---

13. *10; 90; exceed; would not; government bonds; decline; reserves; decline; 10*
14. *exceed*
15. *equal to; buy*

loans are (*increased/reduced*) to make up any deficiency in cash reserves.

16. The economy may be experiencing unemployment due to insufficient aggregate ______________ . To encourage lower interest rates, and thus more borrowing and spending, the Bank of Canada may undertake expansionary monetary policy to (*increase/decrease*) the supply of money. To do this, the Bank of Canada would ________ bonds from/to the public and/or chartered banks. Multiple expansion of bank deposits and loans will only occur, however, if banks are willing to _________ excess reserves and people are willing to ______________ from the banks.

17. The balance sheet of a chartered bank is as follows:

Table 6-7

(CRR = 25%)

Assets		Liabilities	
Cash	$20M	Deposits	$80M
Loans	60M		
	$80M		

If the Bank of Canada buys $5 million in bonds from Stelco and the proceeds of the sale are deposited by Stelco in the above bank, loans from this bank could expand by $ _________ million.

18. If the increase in loans from the bank in paragraph 17 were spent and deposited in another bank, and the process continued indefinitely, the final expansion in bank loans would be $ ___ million.

---

15. *reduced*
16. *demand; increase; buy; lend; borrow*
17. *3.75*
18. *15*

Changing the Cash Reserve Ratio

19. We have seen that the chartered banks must hold a minimum amount of cash based on the CRR. In Chapter 5 we saw that a change in the CRR would affect the composition of a chartered bank's (*assets/liabilities*). If a bank's cash reserves are equal to the legal minimum, loans must be ____________________ if the CRR is increased. This may cause a further (*contraction/expansion*) of loans in the banking system. Although the Bank of Canada does not have the power to change the money supply by changing the CRR, this method is used in other countries.

Changing the Bank Rate

20. As we have seen, the Bank of Canada acts as an agent for the federal government. It is also a bank for the chartered banks. It is possible for chartered banks to borrow from the Bank of Canada. The interest rate charged on loans from the Bank of Canada is called the bank rate. If the bank rate is increased, the cost of borrowing (*increases/decreases*) and the amount of borrowing is likely to (*increase/decrease*). Alternatively, if the bank rate is lowered, then the cost of borrowing (*rises/falls*) and the amount of borrowing is likely to (*rise/fall*).

21. Although Canadian chartered banks borrow extremely infrequently from the Bank of Canada, we can see conceptually that in inflationary periods the Bank of Canada should make the cost of borrowing (*expensive/inexpensive*) by (*increasing/decreasing*) the bank

---

19. *assets; decreased; contraction*
20. *increases; decrease; falls; rise*
21. *expensive; increasing*

rate in order to (*increase/decrease*) borrowing. In periods of high unemployment, the bank rate should be (*increased/decreased*).

Summary

22. In inflationary situations brought on by excessive spending, the appropriate monetary policies for the Bank of Canada appear to be to (*increase/decrease*) the CRR if it had the power, (*increase/decrease*) the bank rate, and (*buy/sell*) government bonds.

23. The appropriate monetary policies for stimulating the economy in periods of unemployment would be to (*buy/sell*) bonds from/to the public, (*increase/decrease*) the bank rate, and (*increase/decrease*) the CRR.

24. An increase in the money supply will likely lead to a (*rise/fall*) in the interest rate, which will (*encourage/discourage*) business to borrow for expenditures on plant, equipment, and inventories. A fall in the interest rate then, will lead to more ____________.

25. Since investment is a component of aggregate demand, a rise in investment leads to a(n) (*increase/decrease*) in aggregate demand and a(n) (*multiple/equal*) (*increase/decrease*) in GNP. If there is unemployment then, a rise in real GNP can be brought about by a (*rise/fall*) in the interest rate due to a (*decline/rise*) in the money supply.

---

21. *decrease; decreased*
22. *increase; increase; sell*
23. *buy; decrease; decrease*
24. *fall; encourage; investment*
25. *increase; multiple increase; fall; rise*

SEVEN

INFLATION, UNEMPLOYMENT, AND TRADE-OFFS

1. Inflation is defined as a persistent and general rise in the prices of goods and services in an economy in a given time period. In previous chapters we argued that price inflation is generated when aggregate demand is (greater/less) than the output that could be produced with all resources fully employed, an output equivalent to (real/money) income. We call this phenomenon demand-pull inflation and depict it as in Figure 7-1.

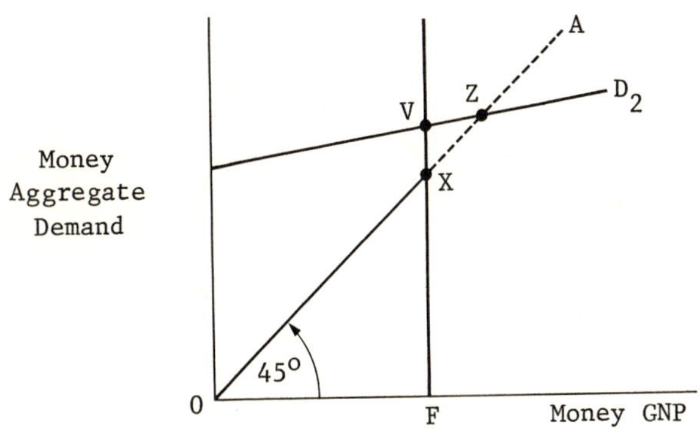

Figure 7-1

2. If OF is potential GNP, then although Z represents a(n) (equilibrium/disequilibrium) GNP, there is an inflationary gap equal to the distance (VX/XZ/OZ). As the economy moves to the

---

1. greater; real
2. equilibrium; VX

right of OF because of (*increasing/decreasing*) aggregate demand, the rate of inflation becomes even greater.

3. Notice, however, that there are no unemployed resources for any GNP level of (OF/OA) or to the right of that level. When there is no unemployment we say that the economy has reached ______________ employment. It is important to note that according to the model we have presented, full employment exists when inflation exists. We will come back to this later.

4. Inflation involves costs to individuals in the Canadian economy. Recall that real income was money income divided by the __________ index. Real income represents purchasing power. An individual whose money income doesn't change in a year in which all prices have risen will find that his real income has (*risen/fallen*). And given that his real income has fallen, his ______________________ power will fall. Old-age pensioners and other groups on fixed incomes can definitely suffer during a(n) ________________________ period.

5. Furthermore, Canada's ability to sell goods and services to foreigners will depend on the prices of these goods and services. The lower the Canadian prices relative to foreign prices, the (*more/less*) goods Canada is likely to sell abroad. If the Canadian economy undergoes an inflationary period (other countries' prices being constant), Canada's competitive strength will (*increase/decrease*) and sales to foreigners should (*rise/fall*), which means Canada's (*imports/exports*) will fall.

---

2. *increasing*
3. *OF; full*
4. *price; fallen; purchasing; inflationary*
5. *more; decrease; fall; exports*

6. If Canada experiences an inflationary period and foreign prices don't change, Canadian consumers will find that prices of domestically produced goods are increasing relative to prices of similar goods produced abroad. Canadians will tend to switch from (*foreign/Canadian*) goods to (*foreign/Canadian*) goods. Additional purchases from foreigners represent increased (*imports/exports*).

7. We previously discovered that GNP = C + I + G + (X - M). If inflation in Canada causes X (exports) to (*increase/decrease*) and M (imports) to (*increase/decrease*), then GNP will (*rise/fall*). And given that a specific level of GNP is associated with a level of employment, inflation may cause GNP to (*increase/decrease*) sufficiently to generate unemployment. Unemployment is a definite cost to Canadian society. It brings about human suffering and loss of real output or real income.

8. We represent an unemployment situation in Figure 7-2.

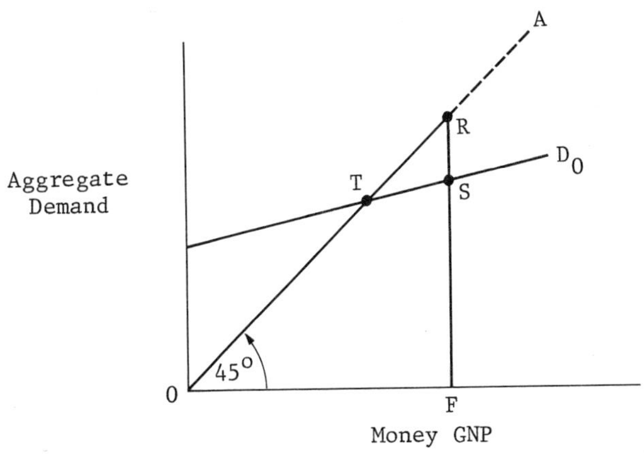

Figure 7-2

---

6. *Canadian; foreign; imports*
7. *decrease; increase; fall; decrease*

Again, we represent potential or ________ employment GNP by the distance OF. The recessionary gap at OF is shown by the distance (*OR/SR/SF*). But recall that between O and F, prices are assumed (*constant/rising*). Given our analysis, any GNP level to the left of F represents (*unemployment/full employment*) with (*constant/rising*) prices.

9. In summary, prices are (*constant/rising*) for levels of GNP greater than OF, (*constant/rising*) to the left of OF, and (*constant/rising*) at a GNP of OF. Unemployment exists for GNP levels to the (*left/right*) of OF.

10. This relationship is represented in Figure 7-3.

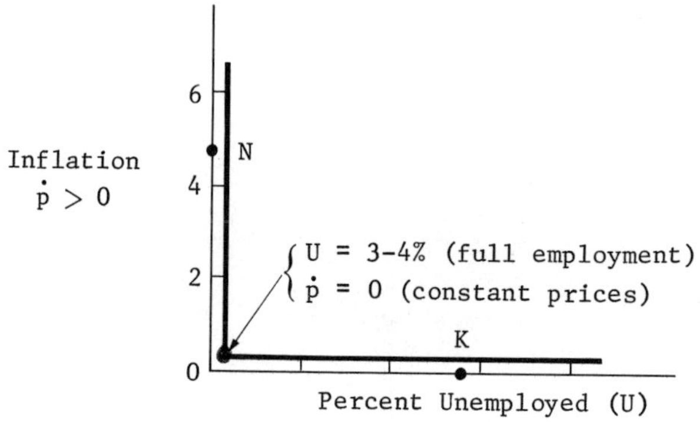

Figure 7-3

Recall that 3-4% unemployment exists at potential GNP. In Figure 7-3 then, we designate the percentage of unemployment in excess of 3-4% as U. At point O, U is (*zero/positive*), and the percentage of price inflation ($\dot{p}$) is (*zero/positive*). To the right of point

---

8. *full; SR; constant; unemployment; constant*
9. *rising; constant; constant; left*
10. *zero; zero*

0, say point K, (unemployment/full employment) exists but prices are (constant/rising). At point N, U is (zero/positive) and $\dot{p}$ is (zero/positive).

11. If we move from K to 0, unemployment (rises/falls) but prices (increase/remain constant). If we move from point N to point 0, price inflation (rises/ceases) and unemployment is (zero/positive).

12. In this model, stopping inflation (from N to 0) generates (some/no) unemployment, and decreasing unemployment (from K to 0) generates (some/no) price inflation.

13. Given that both inflation and unemployment represent costs to society, point (0/N) is definitely superior to points K and (0/N). Therefore, it appears that the government should pursue policies to ensure that the economy remains at point (0/K/N).

14. Unfortunately, the relationship between unemployment and price inflation in Canada may not be that depicted in Figure 7-3. It has tended to be as portrayed by a series of points linked together as in Figure 7-4. Unemployment in this diagram is extremely (high/low) when $\dot{p} = 0$, and price inflation is very (high/low) when $U = 0$.

15. Curve JQL has often been called a Phillips curve. It indicates that as unemployment falls, price inflation (rises/falls). Or, as unemployment (rises/falls), prices fall.

---

10. *unemployment; constant; zero; positive*
11. *falls; remain constant; ceases; zero*
12. *no; no*
13. *0; N; 0*
14. *high; high*
15. *rises; rises*

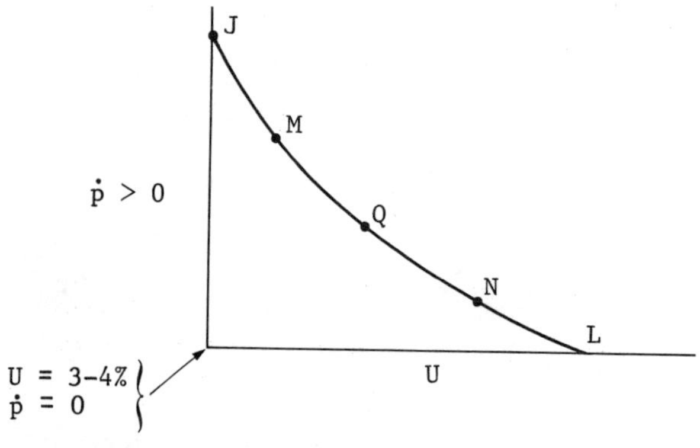

Figure 7-4

16. It is no longer possible to move from point J to 0 or from point L to 0. Only movements along JQL are possible. A movement from J to Q would mean that the Canadian economy experiences (*increased/decreased*) inflation and (*increased/decreased*) unemployment.

17. Government fiscal policies could be used to move from J to Q. In order to reduce inflation, government expenditures should (*rise/fall*) and/or taxes should be (*increased/decreased*). However, a movement from J to Q (*increases/decreases*) unemployment.

18. A movement from L to Q represents (*increasing/decreasing*) unemployment and (*rising/falling*) price inflation. Such a movement could be caused by government expenditures (*increasing/decreasing*) or taxes (*rising/falling*). It is assumed in paragraphs 17 and 18 that the curve JQL is stable in the period when these government fiscal policies are conducted.

---

16. *decreased; increased*
17. *fall; increased; increases*
18. *decreasing; rising; increasing; falling*

19. Therefore, it is possible for inflation and unemployment to co-exist (at points like M, N, and Q in Figure 7-4) if a Phillips curve exists for Canada. But our previous model did not allow for this. In particular, price inflation was (*zero/positive*) when unemployment was high.

20. Thus, we attempt to change our previous model slightly to explain the coexistence of inflation and unemployment. Recall that we gave excessive demand as the explanation for price inflation. Recent evidence suggests that inflation also originates from the supply or cost side. This has been called cost-push inflation. Cost-push inflation results from rising costs associated with the (*supply/demand*) side of the market.

21. In altering our model, let us first take into account the behaviour of suppliers of the factors of production (labour in particular). Labour unions often represent labourers as their collective bargaining agents. If unions negotiate wage increases equal to labour's productivity gains, profits should remain the same and there is no need for businesses to raise prices. Wage increases matched by productivity gains (*should/should not*) generate price inflation.

22. However, labour unions may obtain wage increases that surpass labour's productivity gains. If businesses do not raise their prices, increases greater than the gains in productivity will tend to (*increase/decrease*) profits. On the other hand, if productivity gains are greater than wage increases and prices remain the same, profits will (*rise/fall*).

---

19. *zero*
20. *supply*
21. *should not*
22. *decrease; rise*

23. If wage increases are greater than productivity gains, businessmen will find their profits (*rising/falling*). In order to maintain their profits, they will have to (*increase/decrease*) prices charged to consumers. As more and more businessmen (*raise/lower*) their prices in response to wage increases, price (*inflation/deflation*) is generated.

24. Similarly, if businessmen wish to raise profits when there are no productivity gains, it will likely be necessary for them to ____________________ prices.

25. It now appears that irrespective of the level of aggregate demand, cost increases on the aggregate supply side of the market become price (*increases/decreases*). This type of inflation is called ____________________. As a result, inflation and unemployment (*may/may not*) coexist.

26. Cost-push inflation may also be generated by increases in the prices of imported goods used in the production of domestic goods. For example, if the United States experiences inflation, then the prices of goods that Canada buys from the United States may (*increase/decrease*).

27. Given the rise in prices of imported goods essential to the production of Canadian goods, the cost of producing Canadian goods will (*rise/fall*). In order to maintain their profits, Canadian

---

23. *falling; increase; raise; inflation*
24. *increase*
25. *increases; cost-push; may*
26. *increase*
27. *rise*

businessmen will try to (*increase/decrease*) the prices of the goods that they produce. Consumers may then find the cost of living in Canada (*rising/falling*).

28. Most of the factors previously mentioned determine the position of curve JQL relative to point O. However, the shape of the curve depends on many complex structural aspects of Canada's economy which we shall not deal with here. The importance of the Phillips curve is that it indicates the trade-off between inflation and unemployment. If inflation is (*increased/reduced*), some unemployment may result. Alternatively, for a given reduction in unemployment, a given (*increase/decrease*) in inflation is produced. Such situations constitute difficult dilemmas for government leaders.

---

27. *increase; rising*
28. *reduced; increase*

EIGHT

INTERNATIONAL TRADE, THE BALANCE OF PAYMENTS, AND EXCHANGE MARKETS

The Balance of Payments

1. In Chapter 7, we saw that domestic goals of price stability and unemployment may come into conflict; for example, if the government pursues an expansionary policy to combat (*unemployment/inflation*), prices might be affected in such a way that the rate of inflation (*increases/decreases*).

2. Changes in factors that influence Canada's international trade may also have profound effects for inflation and unemployment in Canada. For example, changes in the quantity of the goods and services that Canadian residents buy from foreign producers, or what are called changes in (*imports/exports*), are likely to change conditions in the Canadian economy.

3. In the chapter concerning multiplier analysis, we saw that an increase in import expenditures will cause GNP to (*rise/fall*) by a(n) (*multiple/equal*) final amount. If the increase in imports is \$5 billion and the MPC is 0.75, GNP will (*rise/fall*) by a final amount of \$ _______ billion.

---

1. *unemployment; increase*
2. *imports*
3. *fall; multiple; fall; 20*

4. Given that GNP has (*risen/fallen*) due to a rise in imports, then it is very likely that Canadian employment will (*rise/fall*).

5. Canadian sales of goods and services, referred to as (*imports/exports*), also figure in Canada's international trade. We previously saw that if exports increase, GNP will (*increase/decrease*) by a(n) (*multiple/equal*) final amount.

6. If GNP (*rises/falls*) because of an increase in exports, then it is very likely that Canadian employment will (*increase/decrease*).

7. If, however, exports increase and full employment exists in Canada, prices will (*increase/decrease*), thereby causing (*inflationary/deflationary*) tendencies.

8. In summary, we have seen that changes in exports and imports can have significant effects on employment and prices in Canada. Given that either imports or exports, expressed as a percentage of GNP, are approximately 25%, then it is clear that major changes in Canada's export and import shares are important determinants of the level of ________________________ and ________________ in Canada.

9. The sale of Canadian goods and services in the world market depends upon several factors: Canadian prices relative to other countries' prices, the income of foreign nations, and preference for Canadian products. It is clear that if Canadian goods and

---

4. *fallen; fall*
5. *exports; increase; multiple*
6. *rises; increase*
7. *increase; inflationary*
8. *employment, prices (either order)*

services have higher prices than competing goods and services produced elsewhere, Canadians will tend to sell (*more/less*) in the world market. If, all other factors constant, foreigners increased their preference for Canadian goods relative to other nations' goods, then Canadian exports would (*increase/decrease*); and if other countries then experienced increases in income, Canadian exports would (*rise/fall*).

10. The purchases of foreign-produced goods and services depend upon Canadian income levels, preference for foreign products, and relative prices of Canadian and foreign-produced goods. A direct relationship between GNP and imports exists, so as GNP increases, imports (*increase/decrease*). And if the prices of Canadian-made products increase relative to prices of foreign-produced substitute goods, imports tend to (*increase/decrease*).

11. The Canadian balance of payments is a record of Canada's transactions with the rest of the world. Unlike Canada's national income accounts, the Canadian balance of payments accounts include financial transactions. For example, if the Canadian government issues a bond series and Americans buy some of the issue, this represents a flow of money into Canada that we call a capital inflow. If Americans buy $10 million in Canadian government securities, the capital ______________ is said to be $ ______ million. Notice that in this transaction the Canadian government issues its liability (the bond) and in return receives an asset (the money). From the Americans' point of view, one asset (money) is exchanged for another asset (the bond). The Canadian bond

---

9. *less; increase; rise*
10. *increase; increase*
11. *inflow; 10*

then, represents a(n) (*asset/liability*) to the Canadian government and a(n) (*asset/liability*) to the Americans.

12. Why might Americans be interested in buying Canadian-issued bonds? If interest yield on Canadian bonds were higher than that on money or American bonds, it would be advantageous (*to buy/not to buy*) Canadian bonds, since they would yield a (*higher/lower*) profit on invested money. If the interest rate on Canadian bonds were 8% and the interest rate on American bonds were 5%, we would expect a capital (*inflow/outflow*) to/from Canada.

13. If Canadians buy other nations' bonds, they are exchanging Canadian assets (money) for foreign bonds. When Canadians pay the U.S. government for a bond, money is flowing out of Canada; this is said to be a capital (*inflow/outflow*).

14. The purchase or sale of bonds does not constitute the only kind of financial transaction across international boundaries. If a British company spends money in Canada to build a plant for producing certain goods, another type of capital (*inflow/outflow*) to/from Canada has taken place, since money is transferred from Great Britain to Canada. We call this capital flow direct investment. When Volvo of Sweden built its new plant in Nova Scotia, this transaction was a capital (*inflow/outflow*) to/from Canada and represented a ______________ investment.

15. Foreigners invest in Canada because they believe that the rate of return on their money will be (*higher/lower*) than the rate of return they would receive if they invested their money elsewhere.

---

11. *liability; asset*
12. *to buy; higher; inflow*
13. *outflow*
14. *inflow; inflow; direct*
15. *higher*

16. Canadians also participate in direct investment in other countries. Canadian banking companies have invested heavily in the West Indies. Such (*direct/indirect*) investments represent capital (*inflow/outflow*) to Canada but capital (*inflow/outflow*) to the West Indies.

17. There are other capital items that are exchanged across Canada's borders. For example, when a Canadian withdraws his money from a Canadian bank and deposits it in a U.S. bank, say in New York, the value of the deposit is a(n) (*asset/liability*) to the U.S. bank and a(n) (*asset/liability*) to the Canadian depository and represents a capital (*inflow/outflow*) to Canada.

18. All transactions in a given accounting period between Canada and the rest of the world are recorded regularly. This is done at least once a year in Canada and includes transactions involving goods and services, and finance. In terms of bookkeeping conventions, Canadian payments to foreigners must equal Canadian receipts. If total Canadian payments to foreigners were $50 million, total Canadian receipts should be $ ________ million.

Current Account

19. Let us look more closely at the subdivisions of the balance of payments transactions (see Table 8-1). The current account basically consists of all transactions involving goods and services. Canada's sales of her goods to foreigners, called merchandise (*imports/exports*), and purchases of goods from

---

16. *direct; outflow; inflow*
17. *liability; asset; outflow*
18. *50*
19. *exports*

foreigners, called (*imports/exports*), appear in the ______________ account. Exports represent receipts to Canadians and imports represent payments to foreigners.

20. It is now possible to define Canada's balance on the merchandise trade account. The balance is the total value of merchandise exports minus the total value of merchandise imports. According to Table 8-1, Canada's merchandise exports were $ __________ million in 1962 and $ __________ million in 1965. Table 8-1 also indicates that payments made to foreigners for merchandise imports were $ __________ million in 1962 and $ __________ million in 1965. As a result, Canada's balance on the merchandise trade account was $ __________ million and $ __________ million in 1962 and 1965 respectively.

21. If the value of exports minus the value of imports is positive, we say that there is a surplus on the balance of Canada's merchandise trade account; if it is negative, Canada has a deficit on the merchandise trade account. In our previous example, Canada has a (*surplus/deficit*) on the merchandise trade account in 1962 and a (*surplus/deficit*) in 1965.

22. We previously mentioned that international transactions involving services represent components of international trade. Services also appear in the current account. Examples are travel expenditures, interest and dividends, and freight and shipping. When a Canadian spends money touring the United States, this represents a payment to Americans. These expenditures will be recorded on the (*receipts/payments*) side of the ______________ account.

---

19. *imports; current*
20. *6,387; 8,745; 6,203; 8,627; 184; 118*
21. *surplus; surplus*
22. *payments; current*

Table 8-1

Canadian Balance of Payments 1962, 1965

(millions of dollars)

CURRENT ACCOUNT

Current Receipts

	1962	1965
Merchandise exports	6,387	8,745
Travel expenditures	562	747
Interest and dividends	202	322
Freight and shipping	509	668
Other current receipts	763	999
Total	8,423	11,481

Current Payments

	1962	1965
Merchandise imports	6,203	8,627
Travel expenditures	605	796
Interest and dividends	783	1,086
Freight and shipping	595	761
Other current payments	1,067	1,341
Total	9,253	12,611

1) CURRENT ACCOUNT BALANCE = CURRENT RECEIPTS - CURRENT PAYMENTS

Source: Statistics Canada

Table 8-1 (Cont.)

Canadian Balance of Payments 1962, 1965

(millions of dollars)

CAPITAL ACCOUNT

Receipts

	1962	1965
Direct investment	505	535
Trade in long-term Canadian securities (net)	359	631
Trade in long-term foreign securities (net)	---	---
Other long-term capital (net)	---	---
Short-term capital movements (net)	296	424
Total	1,160	1,590

Payments

	1962	1965
Direct investment	105	125
Trade in long-term Canadian securities (net)	---	---
Trade in long-term foreign securities (net)	65	85
Other long-term capital (net)	6	92
Short-term capital movements	---	---
Total	176	302

2) CAPITAL ACCOUNT BALANCE = CAPITAL RECEIPTS - CAPITAL PAYMENTS

Source: Statistics Canada

Table 8-1 (Cont.)

SUMMARY OF BALANCE OF INTERNATIONAL PAYMENTS

Current Account Balance	1962	1965
1962: (8,423 - 9,253) =	- 830 (deficit)	
1965: (11,481 - 12,611) =		- 1,130 (deficit)
Capital Account Balance		
1962: (1,160 - 176) =	+ 984 (surplus)	
1965: (1,590 - 302) =		+ 1,288 (surplus)
Balance of Payments		
Deficit(-) or Surplus(+)	+ 154	+ 158
Change in holdings of gold and official foreign exchange	+ 154	+ 158

3) CHANGE IN GOLD AND OFFICIAL FOREIGN RESERVES = BALANCE OF PAYMENTS DEFICIT OR SURPLUS

Source: Statistics Canada

In a sense, when Canadians travel abroad, payments to foreigners for tourist services represent (*imports/exports*) in the Canadian current account.

23. Alternatively, when foreigners visit Canada and spend money, this represents an (*import/export*) of tourist services and appears as a (*receipt/payment*) in Canada's ________________ account. The same type of analysis applies to shipping services and to interest and dividend payments and receipts. When a Canadian company pays

---

22. *imports*
23. *export; receipt; current*

dividends to British shareholders, this represents a (*receipt/payment*); when CNR ships goods from Chicago to Toronto for a U.S. firm, this transaction appears as a (*receipt/payment*) in Canada's __________________ account.

24. Once all transactions of goods and services (along with a few other items shown in Table 8-1) are classified as payments or receipts, we may define Canada's balance on the current account. Exports of goods and services, payments received for shipping or interest, etc., appear on the (*receipts/payments*) side, whereas imports of goods and services, payments to foreigners for shipping, etc., appear on the (*receipts/payments*) side. The total value of current account receipts minus the total value of current account payments is called the balance on the current account. We can see from Table 8-1 that Canada had a (*surplus/deficit*) on its current account for both 1962 and 1965. In other words, Canadians were buying (*more/fewer*) goods and services than they were selling in these years.

Capital Account

25. Recall that various financial transactions occur internationally. When Americans invest in new buildings and equipment in Canada, this is considered a direct investment in Canada and represents a capital (*inflow/outflow*) to Canada. Direct investment in Canada appears on the (*receipts/payments*) side of what is called the long-term capital account.

---

23. *payment; receipt; current*
24. *receipts; payments; deficit; more*
25. *inflow; receipts*

26. Canadian investment in the West Indies represents a capital (*inflow/outflow*) to Canada and hence appears on the (*receipts/payments*) side of the long-term capital account. Such direct investments are considered long-term capital assets because they are long-term propositions. In 1962, foreigners invested directly $ ________ million in Canada.

27. Government and private bonds of greater than five-year maturity are called long-term bonds. If Americans buy $8 million in ten-year Province of Ontario bonds, this transaction appears as a (*receipt/payment*) in the long-term capital account. According to Table 8-1, $ ________ million in Canadian securities was sold to foreigners in 1965. On the other hand, Canadians purchased $ ________ million in foreign securities in 1965.

28. In addition to long-term capital movements, there are what we call short-term capital movements - sales and purchases of securities and assets of less than five years to maturity and the movement of bank deposits from one country to another. In 1962 Canada borrowed or received on a short-term basis $ ________ million from foreigners. The sale of short-term securities to foreigners is a(n) (*asset/liability*) to Canadians and a(n) (*asset/liability*) to foreigners.

29. By totaling long and short-term capital movements on the receipts and payments sides of the account, and subtracting total payments from total receipts, the capital account balance is obtained. In 1962, capital receipts were $ __________ million while payments

---

26. *outflow; payments; 505*
27. *receipt; 631; 85*
28. *296; liability; asset*
29. *1,160*

were $ ________ million, giving a balance on capital account of $ ________ million. Since this is a (*positive/negative*) amount, the balance on capital account was a (*surplus/deficit*).

30. Whether the overall balance of payments is a surplus or deficit depends upon the net result of the balances on current and capital accounts. In 1965 the current account balance was a ____________ of $ __________ million, while the capital account balance was a ________________ of $ __________ million. The net result is $ ________ million, which is a (*surplus/deficit*).

31. Although Canada paid out more than was received for goods and services in 1965, this was offset by a net (*inflow/outflow*) of foreign exchange on the ________________ account.

32. The 1965 balance of payments surplus of $ ________ million is added to Canada's holdings of foreign exchange or gold, which can be used for international transactions. If the balance of payments were a deficit, the official holdings of gold and foreign exchange would (*decrease/remain the same*). Financing a deficit this way is analagous to an individual's dipping into his savings. A $100 million deficit in the balance of payments (*increases/reduces*) gold or foreign exchange by $ ________ million.

33. An increase in foreign exchange holdings with a zero balance on current account implies a ________________ on the ______________ account.

---

29. *176; 984; positive; surplus*
30. *deficit; 1,130; surplus; 1,288; 158; surplus*
31. *inflow; capital*
32. *158; decrease; reduces; 100*
33. *surplus; capital*

34. A decrease in foreign exchange holdings with a surplus on current account implies a ________________ on ________________ account that is (*greater than/equal to*) the surplus on current account.

35. Alternatively, foreigners may run down their reserve accounts (gold plus foreign currency) in order to pay Canadians. If this occurs, reserves of __________ and ________________ ________________ will (*increase/decrease*) in the Bank of Canada.

36. Table 8-1 shows that for 1962, changes in official holdings of gold and foreign exchange were $ ________ million, which is precisely equal to the (*surplus/deficit*) in Canada's balance of payments for that year.

Foreign Exchange Markets

37. When a foreigner buys Canadian goods, he needs to obtain Canadian dollars in order to pay the seller (assuming that the Canadian would not accept foreign currency). Similarly, if a Canadian buys goods from an American, he must obtain (*U.S./Canadian*) dollars in order to pay for the goods (assuming the American dislikes foreign currency). When a Canadian buys a British government bond, he usually must convert his Canadian dollars to pounds sterling. The price of one currency in terms of another is called the <u>foreign exchange rate</u>. For example, one pound sterling may cost $3 in Canadian currency. Thus a British customer will obtain (*3; 1; 1/3*)

---

34. *deficit; capital; greater than*
35. *gold; foreign currency; increase*
36. *154; surplus*
37. *U.S.; 3*

Canadian dollar(s) for each pound sterling, while a Canadian must pay \$3 to obtain *(1; 3; 1/3)* pound(s).

38. Alternatively, the exchange rate may be expressed in terms of the foreign currency; one Canadian dollar is worth £1/3. The latter value is the reciprocal of the dollar value of one pound. Both represent the same exchange rate. If one U.S. dollar is worth 1.05 Canadian dollars, it follows that one Canadian dollar is worth approximately *(0.95/1.00/1.05)* U.S. dollar(s).

39. We wish to look at the factors that determine the international demand and supply of Canadian dollars. When Canadians sell goods and services and long-term capital to foreigners, foreigners have a demand for Canadian dollars. For example, if a Canadian pulp and paper company sells its goods to the New York Times, the Times must exchange U.S. dollars for ________________ dollars. This creates a *(demand/supply)* for Canadian dollars. Hence all *(imports/exports)* of goods and services represent *(supply/demand)* for Canadian dollars. Similarly, if Germans buy Canadian companies or securities, they must exchange Deutschemarks for Canadian dollars. All long-term capital inflows give rise to *(demand/supply)* for/of Canadian dollars.

40. On the other hand, when Canadians buy goods from foreigners, or what we have called *(imports/exports)*, they need to exchange Canadian dollars for various foreign currencies.

41. If Canadians buy French-produced wine, Canadian importers must exchange dollars for francs. If Canadians invest in Britain, a

---

37. *1*
38. *0.95*
39. *Canadian; demand; exports; demand; demand*
40. *imports*

transaction representing a capital (*inflow/outflow*) to Canada, they must buy ______________________________ at a given exchange rate. And if \$1 Canadian is exchanged for £1/3, then in order to obtain £2, the Canadian must pay \$ (*6/3/1*). All imports of goods and services and all long-term capital outflows create (*supply/demand*) for pounds sterling. But in the process of demanding pounds sterling, Canadians are supplying Canadian dollars.

42. Let us represent in diagrams the demand for and supply of Canadian dollars for international transactions. The lines drawn in the following diagrams are not to be confused with the aggregate demand and aggregate supply lines in previous chapters. For both demand and supply of Canadian dollars we measure the quantity of Canadian dollars on the horizontal axis. The vertical axis represents the price of one Canadian dollar in terms of a foreign currency (say, pounds sterling).

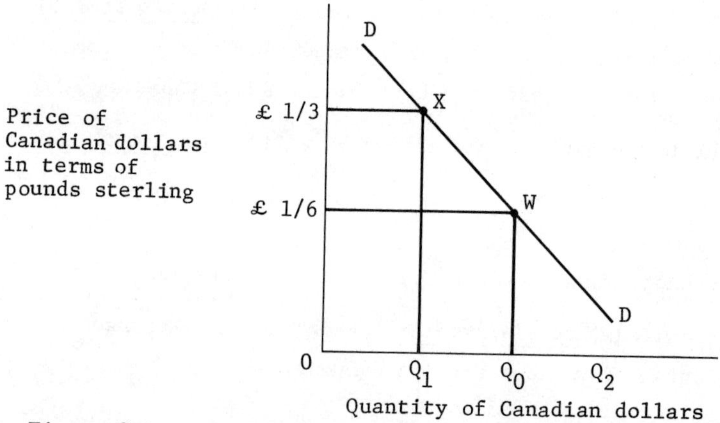

Figure 8-1

---

41. *outflow; pounds sterling; 6; demand*

43. By deriving a demand curve for Canadian dollars, we hope to ascertain the effect on the quantity of Canadian dollars when the value of the exchange rate (the price of Canadian dollars in terms of pounds sterling) changes. The demand curve for Canadian dollars (DD line) is downward sloping. Hence, the lower the price of the Canadian dollar in terms of pounds, the (*greater/less*) will be the quantity of Canadian dollars demanded. Alternatively, the higher the price of Canadian dollars (expressed in terms of pounds) the (*greater/less*) will be the quantity demanded.

44. Although this might be difficult to see at first, think of what a fall in the number of pounds required to buy one Canadian dollar would mean to a British consumer of Canadian goods. If the exchange rate was originally £1/3 per $1 Canadian, then in order to purchase five pounds of Canadian bacon costing $3, the British consumer would have to exchange £ (*1/3; 3; 1*) for $3 Canadian. If the exchange rate fell to £1/6 per $1 Canadian, the five pounds of bacon worth $3 could be obtained by exchanging £ (*1/2; 1; 1/3*) for $3 Canadian. A fall in the pounds sterling cost per Canadian dollar is likely to (*increase/decrease*) the quantity of Canadian dollars demanded.

45. Given that Canadian bacon represents Canadian (*imports/exports*) to Britain, we can see that a fall in the exchange rate will (*increase/decrease*) the quantity of Canadian dollars demanded. This is shown in Figure 8-1.

46. Similarly, capital inflows will constitute demand for Canadian dollars. When a foreigner buys a Canadian bond, he must exchange

---

43. *greater; less*
44. *1; 1/2; increase*
45. *exports; increase*

his currency for ________________ . If the price of dollars in terms of his currency falls, then the price of the bond has effectively (*increased/decreased*). Hence he, along with others, can afford (*more/less*) Canadian bonds. The more the demand for Canadian bonds, the (*greater/less*) the demand for Canadian dollars.

47. Both exports and capital inflows constitute (*demand/supply*) for Canadian dollars. As the exchange rate falls, exports and capital inflows are likely to (*increase/decrease*) and the quantity demanded for dollars will (*increase/decrease*). Such an occurrence is depicted by a movement along the demand curve in Figure 8-1 from point X to point W. When the exchange rate falls, there is a(n) (*increase/decrease*) in the quantity of dollars demanded, portrayed by a (*movement along/shift in*) the demand curve.

48. Changes in all other factors that influence Canadian exports, such as other nations' income, and preference for Canadian goods, will shift the demand curve for Canadian dollars. When foreigners change their taste for a certain Canadian product, we may depict this situation by a (*movement along/shift in*) the demand curve.

49. If foreigners' income increases, their demand for Canadian goods will (*increase/decrease*). (*Imports/Exports*) will then increase, and the change creates a(n) (*increased/decreased*) (*supply/demand*) for Canadian dollars. This is depicted as a shift to the (*left/right*) in Figure 8-2.

---

46. *dollars; decreased; more; greater*
47. *demand; increase; increase; increase; movement along*
48. *shift in*
49. *increase; Exports; increased demand; right*

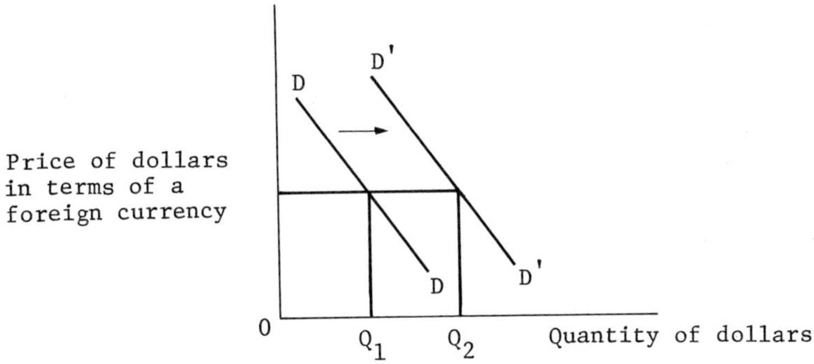

Figure 8-2

50. Alternatively, if foreigners' income falls, the demand for Canadian dollars (*increases/decreases*) and so the demand curve shifts to the (*left/right*).

51. By constructing a supply curve for dollars, we wish to explain the effect on the quantity supplied when the exchange rate changes. As drawn in Figure 8-3, the supply of Canadian dollars tends to be upward sloping; the higher the price of the Canadian dollar in terms of pounds sterling, the (*greater/less*) will be the quantity of Canadian dollars supplied. The lower the exchange rate, the (*lower/higher*) will be the quantity offered to the market. Again, this is not obvious at first. Recall, however, that imports of goods and services and long-term capital inflows represent factors that generated supplies of Canadian dollars. For example, if a Canadian buys a British sports car from a British auto company, he must (*demand/supply*) Canadian dollars in order to obtain (demand) ______________________________. Say the exchange rate

---

50. *decreases; left*
51. *greater; lower; supply; pounds sterling*

was £1/3 per $1 Canadian and the Canadian had to pay £1,000 for the car. Then, he must exchange $ <u>(*3,000/1,000/333*)</u> in order to pay the British auto company £1,000. If the exchange rate fell to £1/6 per $1 Canadian, he must exchange $ <u>(*6,000/3,000/1,000*)</u> to obtain £1,000. In terms of dollars, the price of the car has <u>(*risen/fallen*)</u>.

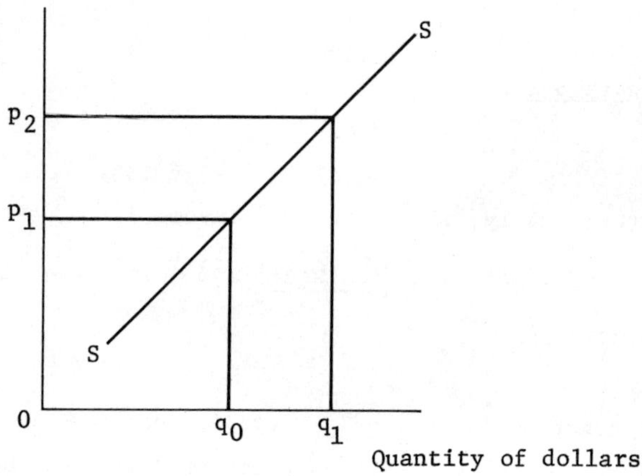

Figure 8-3

52. If the exchange rate falls then, the Canadian dollar price of British cars will <u>(*rise/fall*)</u> and so the quantity demand for cars will tend to fall. Imports of U.K. cars into Canada would <u>(*rise/fall*)</u> and in turn <u>(*more/fewer*)</u> Canadian dollars would be supplied.

53. From Figure 8-3, we see that as the price of Canadian dollars rises, the quantity of imports <u>(*rises/decreases*)</u> and so the quantity of dollars supplied <u>(*increases/decreases*)</u>. When the

---

51. *3,000; 6,000; risen*
52. *rise; fall; fewer*
53. *rises; increases*

exchange rate changes, this is depicted as a movement along the supply line.

54. Previously we saw that the quantity of imports was influenced by the level of Canadian GNP and by taste for foreign goods. If either or both of these factors change, then the quantity of imports will change. More specifically, if Canadian GNP rises, imports will (*increase/decrease*). This in turn will increase the (*supply/demand*) of dollars.

55. Changes in factors influencing imports, other than the exchange rate, cause the supply curve for dollars to shift. For example, if Canadian GNP rises, the supply curve for dollars will ____________ to the (*left/right*).

Exchange Rate Systems

56. If the forces of demand and supply for Canadian dollars were allowed to determine the exchange rate, there would be an exchange rate at which demand equaled supply. Such an exchange rate is called an equilibrium rate.

57. In terms of Figure 8-4, OB represents an equilibrium exchange rate, since the quantity ____________________ equals the quantity ____________________ , an amount represented by OQ_0. However, OC (*is/is not*) an equilibrium rate because demand and supply (*are/are not*) equal. In fact, the quantity supplied is (*greater/less*)

---

54. *increase; supply*
55. *shift; right*
57. *supplied, demanded (either order); is not; are not; greater*

than the quantity demanded. In this case, since an equilibrium (*exists/does not exist*), adjustments in the foreign exchange market will occur.

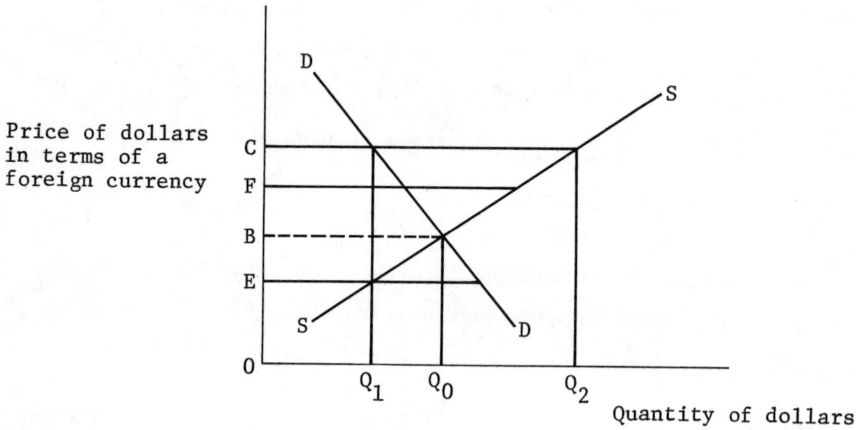

Figure 8-4

58. At an exchange rate of OC, suppliers of Canadian dollars find that they cannot find sufficient buyers for Canadian dollars. So the suppliers react by lowering the price of Canadian dollars, say to OF. At OF, ______________ is still greater than ______________ . But notice that a change in the exchange rate from OC to OF has (*increased/decreased*) the demand for Canadian dollars slightly and (*increased/decreased*) the supply of dollars. OF is not an equilibrium rate. The suppliers will continue to lower the exchange rate to ______ , which represents an equilibrium rate. At this point, both buyers and sellers are satisfied.

59. We could just as easily have analyzed the reaction of the market at an exchange rate of OE. At this exchange rate, quantity

---

57. *does not exist*
58. *supply; demand; increased; decreased; OB*

__________________ is greater than quantity __________________ and so an __________________ does not exist in this market.

60. Given that the quantity demanded is (*greater/less*) than the quantity supplied, buyers will tend to bid up the exchange rate. As the rate increases, quantity demanded (*rises/falls*) and quantity supplied (*rises/falls*). This process will continue until an equilibrium is reached at ______ .

61. A foreign exchange market in which the foreign exchange rate is determined solely by changes in demand and supply is called a flexible exchange rate system. Under such a system, the government does not intervene in the market to change or maintain a given value of the rate. From 1971, Canada for the most part allowed its foreign exchange rate to be determined largely by the forces of demand and supply. Thus Canada has a __________________ exchange rate system. A flexible or floating exchange rate system was described in the previous analysis. Specifically, OB in Figure 8-4 would have been the exchange rate in a flexible exchange system.

62. Between 1962 and 1970, Canada did not allow its exchange rate to fluctuate freely. Instead, the government set a value which was not allowed to change. Such an exchange system generates a fixed exchange rate. An exchange rate that is not allowed to fluctuate freely then, is called a ______________ exchange rate.

---

59. *demanded; supplied; equilibrium*
60. *greater; falls; rises; OB*
61. *flexible*
62. *fixed*

63. Figure 8-5 indicates that the government of Canada wishes to fix, or peg, its exchange rate at the level OG.

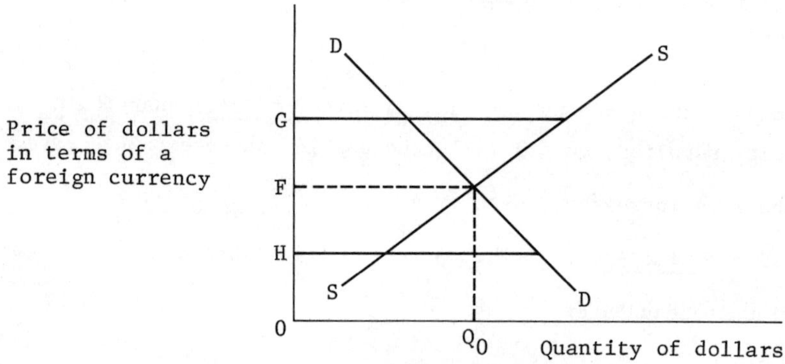

Figure 8-5

The DD and SS curves represent the free market demand and supply curves for Canadian dollars. Hence, the government-pegged rate is (*above/below*) the rate that would prevail under a flexible exchange rate system. The free market equilibrium rate is represented by (*OH/OF/OG*). From the diagram, it can be clearly seen that OG is not an equilibrium rate, because the quantity (*supplied/demanded*) is greater than the quantity ________________. We saw previously that if the market were free to react, the rate would fall from OG to (*OF/OH*).

64. But under a fixed exchange rate system, the government is committed to maintain the rate OG. The only way it can do this is to intervene in the market. For example, we have noted that the quantity supplied is (*greater/less*) than the quantity demanded at

---

63. *above; OF; supplied; demanded; OF*
64. *greater*

exchange rate OG. Deficient (*supply/demand*) exists at rate OG. The government then, participates in the foreign exchange rate market by (*buying/selling*) Canadian dollars to fill the deficiency in (*supply/demand*).

65. Alternatively, if the Government pegged the rate at OH, the rate would be (*above/below*) the equilibrium rate of ______ . Since the quantity __________________ is greater than the quantity __________________ at OH, it would be necessary for the government to (*buy/sell*) Canadian dollars in order to satisfy the deficiency in (*supply/demand*) of dollars.

The Balance of Payments and the Exchange Rate

66. In Figure 8-6, we see that at the exchange rate OE the supply of dollars (OQ_2) is (*greater/less*) than the demand for dollars (OQ_1).

Price of dollars in terms of a foreign currency

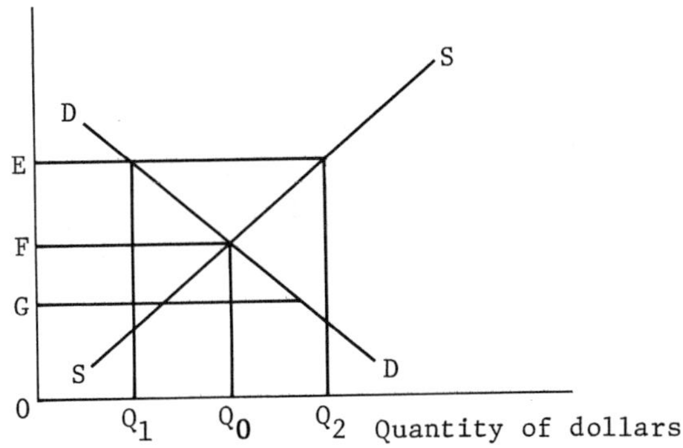

Figure 8-6

---

64. *demand; buying; demand*
65. *below; OF; demanded; supplied; sell; supply*
66. *greater*

Since the supply of dollars is determined by imports and capital outflows and the demand for dollars is determined by exports and capital inflows, then at an exchange rate of OE the balance of payments would be in a (*deficit/surplus*) position.

67. At OF, demand is (*greater than/equal to*) supply and so the balance of payments is in an ____________________ position. At OG, demand is (*greater than/equal to*) supply and so there is a (*surplus/deficit*) in the balance of payments.

68. Suppose that the economy was originally at an equilibrium balance of payments position at exchange rate OF and the demand curve for dollars then shifted to the right as is depicted in Figure 8-7. After the shift, at the exchange rate OF, the demand for dollars, at point T, is (*greater/less*) than the supply, at point Z. At an exchange rate of OF then, the balance of payments is in a (*surplus/deficit*) position.

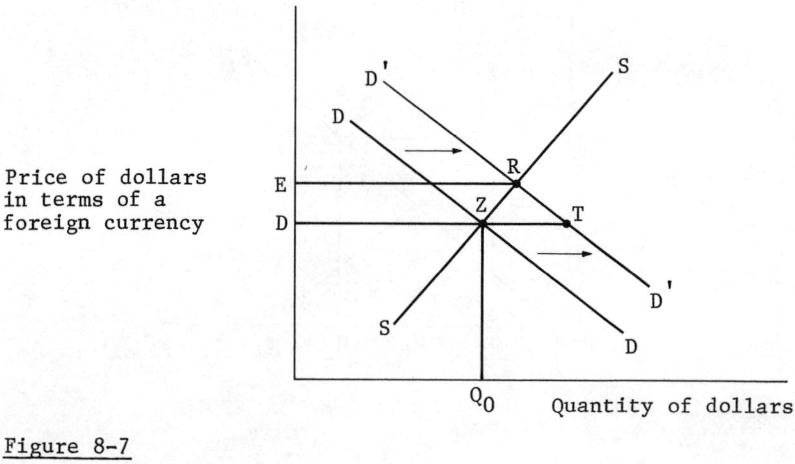

Figure 8-7

---

66. *deficit*
67. *equal to; equilibrium; greater than; surplus*
68. *greater; surplus*

69. If the exchange rate were free to move, or a ________________ exchange rate system existed, the exchange rate would eventually move from OF to *(OE/OG)*, at which a new ________________ point R exists and so the balance of payments would again be in a(n) *(deficit/equilibrium)* position.

70. Once a pegged rate is established, it is possible for the government of Canada to change the rate to a new level. Say the original rate was OG, as shown in Figure 8-8. At this exchange rate, a *(surplus/deficit)* balance of payments situation exists. Now the government decides to change the rate to OH. Lowering the pegged rate is called devaluation. Say OG represented an exchange rate of £1/3 per $1 Canadian and OH represented a rate of £1/6 per $1 Canadian. We see in Figure 8-8 that the quantity of dollars demanded at a rate of OG is *($OQ_3/OQ_2/OQ_1$)* and that the quantity demanded at rate OH is *($OQ_4/OQ_3/OQ_2$)*. The quantity demanded has *(increased/decreased)*.

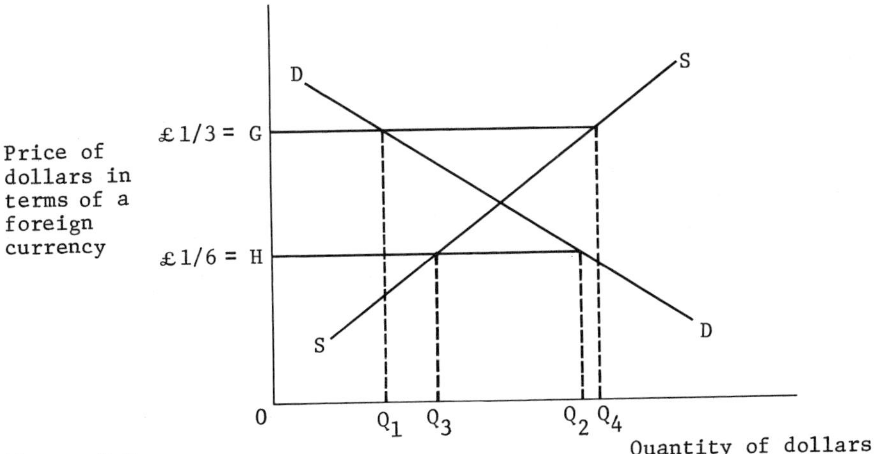

Figure 8-8

---

69. *flexible; OE; equilibrium; equilibrium*
70. *deficit; OQ_1; OQ_2; increased*

71. We saw that the demand for Canadian dollars was determined by the (imports/exports) of goods and services and the long-term capital (inflows/outflows). If the rate is devalued from OG to OH, we see that (imports/exports) transactions are stimulated and so the (supply/demand) for Canadian dollars (increases/decreases).

72. On the other hand, a change in the rate from OG to OH also has the effect of (increasing/decreasing) the supply of Canadian dollars from ($OQ_4/OQ_2/OQ_3$) to ($OQ_3/OQ_1/OQ_2$). If the quantity supplied has (risen/fallen) due to devaluation, this means that imports have (risen/fallen), since imports determine the quantity of Canadian dollars supplied.

73. Thus, we have seen that a devaluation encourages (imports/exports) and discourages (imports/exports) by making (imports/exports) dearer to Canadians and (imports/exports) cheaper to foreigners.

74. If the government changed the rate from OH to OG, it would be appreciating, or revaluing, the exchange rate. Such a procedure would (increase/decrease) the demand for Canadian dollars and (increase/decrease) the supply of Canadian dollars. We know that as a consequence, (imports/exports) will become cheaper and so their quantity will (increase/decrease), and that (imports/exports) will become dearer and so their quantity will (increase/decrease).

---

71. *exports; inflows; exports; demand; increases*
72. *decreasing;* OQ_4*;* OQ_3*; fallen; fallen*
73. *exports; imports; imports; exports*
74. *decrease; increase; imports; increase; exports; decrease*

75. Since devaluation ______________________ exports, and greater exports mean a higher GNP and higher employment, devaluation might be used to ______________ unemployment. Similarly, appreciation might be used to ________________ inflation since it ______________ exports and thus reduces aggregate demand.

76. Notice also that devaluation and appreciation affect GNP through the effect on imports: devaluation _________________ imports and appreciation ______________________ imports.

---

75. *increases; reduce; reduce; reduces*
76. *reduces; increases*

APPENDIX

In this section we will present various models of aggregate demand that represent more complex relationships than were discussed in Chapters 2 and 3. We have not included them in the main body of the text since students and teachers may not wish to include more complex relations in an introductory macroeconomics course.

Throughout the analysis that follows we will assume that the price level is constant.

A Review

1. In previous chapters, we saw that consumption expenditures were dependent on the level of national income, or GNP. For example, the following schedule represents a hypothetical consumption relationship.

Table A-1

GNP	Consumption
$ 0 billion	$ 10 billion
50	50
100	90
150	130

Autonomous consumption expenditures (*depend/do not depend*) on the level of GNP and in this case are $ (*0/10/130*) billion. However, some consumption expenditures are dependent on the level of GNP. These are called induced consumption expenditures. Specifically,

1. *do not depend; 10*

when GNP increases to \$50 billion, consumption increases by \$ (40/50/0) billion. The marginal propensity to consume then, is (5/0.8/1). In Table A-1 we see that the MPC is (increasing/decreasing/constant) for all increases in income and consumption.

2. Assuming consumption expenditures are the only component of aggregate demand, if autonomous consumption increased, GNP would increase by a(n) (multiple/equal) amount.

3. The specific amount by which GNP would change depends upon the size of the multiplier, which can be calculated by using the expression ($\frac{1}{1 - MPC}$ / $\frac{1}{MPC}$). If the MPC were 0.8, the value of the multiplier would be ______ .

4. If aggregate demand included autonomous investment expenditures as well as the consumption expenditures previously described, an increase in autonomous investment expenditures would also cause GNP to (increase/decrease) by a(n) (multiple/equal) amount.

5. Furthermore, we know that the value of the multiplier for changes in autonomous investment expenditures is (different from/equal to) the value of the multiplier for changes in autonomous consumption. For example, if the MPC were 0.9 and autonomous investment decreased by \$10 million, GNP would fall by \$ ________ million.

6. Similarly, if the components of aggregate demand were to include investment, government expenditures, exports, and imports, <u>and</u> as

---

1. *40; 0.8; constant*
2. *multiple*
3. *1/(1-MPC); 5*
4. *increase; multiple*
5. *equal to; 100*

long as they were all autonomous, then the value of the multiplier would be ($\frac{1}{1 - MPC}$ / $\frac{1}{MPC}$).

7. Generally speaking, the relationships described in paragraphs 1 to 6 do not represent real-world behaviour. We wish to show the reader the effects on the value of the multiplier of making both investment and import expenditures dependent on the level of GNP.

Investment Relationship

8. Assume that consumption is dependent on the level of GNP but government expenditures, exports, and imports are autonomous; that is, they (*depend/do not depend*) on the level of GNP. If investment expenditures are dependent on GNP, then they (*are/are not*) autonomous. In fact, this type of investment relationship is called induced investment because it depends on the level of ________ .

9. Some economists believe that the level of GNP represents the general level of business profits. According to this analysis, the higher the level of GNP, the (*higher/lower*) the level of profits businessmen expect.

10. We suggested previously that if expected profits increase, investment expenditures are likely to be (*higher/lower*). Since expected profits are generally thought to be dependent on the level of GNP, investment expenditures are also dependent on ________ .

---

6. *1/(1-MPC)*
8. *do not depend; are not; GNP*
9. *higher*
10. *higher; GNP*

11. A hypothetical GNP and investment expenditures relationship is given in Table A-2.

Table A-2

GNP	Investment
$ 0 billion	$0 billion
10	1
20	2
40	4

When the GNP is $10 billion, investment expenditures are $ (*0/1/2*) billion. When GNP changes from $0 billion to $10 billion, investment changes by $ ______ billion. Similarly, if GNP changes from $10 billion to $20 billion, investment (*increases/decreases*) by $ ______ billion.

12. The change in investment expressed as a proportion of the change in GNP is called the marginal propensity to invest. If the change in investment is $1 billion and the change in GNP is $10 billion, then the marginal propensity to invest (MPI) is equal to (*1/0.1/10*).

13. The information contained in Table A-2 has been sketched in Figure A-1. From Figure A-1, we can see that the MPI is (*constant/changing*) and is equal to (*1/0.1/10*).

14. The MPI is represented by the slope of the investment line in Figure A-1. In this case the slope is (*constant/changing*) and has a value of ______ .

---

11. *1; 1; increases; 1*
12. *0.1*
13. *constant; 0.1*
14. *constant; 0.1*

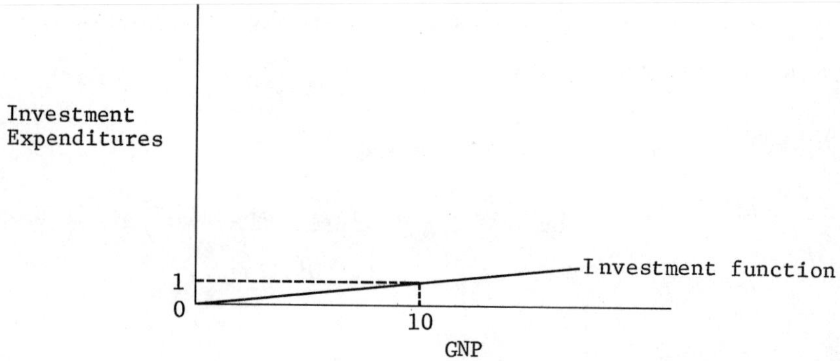

Figure A-1

15. A model of aggregate demand that includes induced consumption and induced investment will yield a different value of the multiplier than a model with only induced consumption. In particular, if induced investment is included (i.e., MPI is greater than zero), the value of the multiplier (*will/will not*) be the same as when the MPI is zero.

16. Let us investigate the way in which the value of the multiplier will change. We previously saw that as the value of the MPC increased, the value of the multiplier ____________________ . This was because consumers were spending a (*greater/lesser*) proportion of their additional income for additional consumption goods.

17. Introducing induced investment and the MPI into our model is conceptually similar to increasing the value of the MPC. If the MPI is introduced into a model, the value of the multiplier will (*increase/decrease*).

---

15. *will not*
16. *increased; greater*
17. *increase*

18. A model in which investment expenditures were autonomous yielded a value for the multiplier of ($\frac{1}{1-MPC}$ / $\frac{1}{MPC}$). So when investment is induced and included in a model (MPI greater than zero), then the new value of the multiplier will be (*greater/less*) than ($\frac{1}{1-MPC}$ / $\frac{1}{MPC}$).

19. More specifically, when the MPI is introduced into the model, the new value of the multiplier is given by the expression $\frac{1}{1-(MPC+MPI)}$. If the MPC is 0.8 and the MPI is 0.1, then the value of the multiplier is (*10/5/3.3*). This multiplier is greater than our previous multiplier of $\frac{1}{1-MPC}$, which in this case has the value of (*1/5/1.25*).

Import Relationship

20. Empirical evidence suggests that imports into Canada bear a positive relationship to GNP. Specifically, if Canada's GNP increases, imports of foreign-produced goods and services will (*increase/decrease*). This is because the ability to purchase imports increases as GNP (*increases/decreases*). Imports that depend on the value of GNP are called induced imports.

21. Suppose GNP and import expenditures are given by the schedule in Table A-3.

---

18. *1/(1-MPC); greater; 1/(1-MPC)*
19. *10; 5*
20. *increase; increases*

Table A-3

GNP	Imports
$ 0 billion	$0 billion
5	1
10	2
20	4

As GNP increases from $0 billion to $5 billion, imports (*increase/decrease*) by $ ______ billion. The increase in imports expressed as a proportion of the increase in GNP is called the marginal propensity to import (MPM). For the preceding example, the MPM has a value of ______ .

22. We notice that in Table A-3 the MPM is assumed to be (*constant/increasing*).

23. The data in Table A-3 are illustrated in Figure A-2. The slope of the import line is equal to the value of the MPM. In this case, the slope is (*constant/changing*) and has a value of ______ .

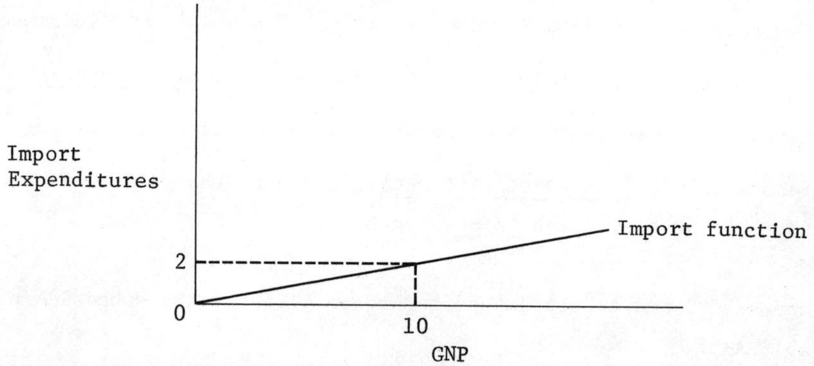

Figure A-2

---

21. *increase; 1; 0.2*
22. *constant*
23. *constant; 0.2*

24. If we assume a model of aggregate demand in which there are induced consumption and induced imports while investment, government, and export expenditures are autonomous, the value of the multiplier will be different from the value of the multiplier for a model in which the only induced expenditure is consumption. If induced imports are included (i.e., the MPM is greater than zero), the value of the multiplier (*will/will not*) be the same as when MPM is zero.

25. We know that if the MPC decreases, the value of the multiplier (*increases/decreases*). When the MPM is introduced into a model, it is conceptually similar to decreases in the MPC. The reason for this is that if Canadians spend more of each dollar in income on foreign goods, less income will be available for spending on Canadian-produced goods. If the MPM appears in our model and is greater than zero, the new value of the multiplier will be (*greater/less*) than the value of the multiplier when the MPM was not included.

26. The value of the multiplier in a model in which the MPM is 0 was measured by the formula $\frac{1}{1-MPC}$. When the MPM is greater than zero, the value of the multiplier becomes $\frac{1}{1-(MPC-MPM)}$. If the MPC is 0.8 and the MPM is 0.2, the value of the multiplier is (*1.67/2.5/5*). If the MPM is 0 and the MPC is 0.8, then the value of the multiplier is (*1.25/5/4*).

---

24. *will not*
25. *decreases; less*
26. *2.5; 5*

27. Finally, if we construct a model of aggregate demand in which positive MPC, MPI, and MPM values exist, the value of the multiplier becomes $\frac{1}{1-(MPC+MPI-MPM)}$. If MPC is 0.8, the MPI is 0.1, and the MPM is 0.2, then the multiplier has the value of (5/2.5/3.3).

---

27. 3.3